Built For More

Living a life of Purpose in a Crazy World

Abimbola Olumuyiwa

Dedication

Dear reader, I am dedicating this book to you; because there is so much more on the inside of you and the world desperately needs what you have to offer. You are worth every letter of every word of every sentence of every page in this book. You are worth all the effort that went into writing this book. Don't you ever minimize your worth.

Do me a favor and personalize all of the above to yourself. You are reason enough; more than enough.

Acknowledgement

I need to acknowledge some very special people in my life. You all are amazing and without you one way or the other, this book would have never become a reality.

Kayode Olumuyiwa – My darling husband who has always nudged me from day one to be a better version of myself daily. You are heaven-sent and I am so blessed that I get to do life with you. Thank you for always supporting my dreams. Thank you for being my soul-mate. Thank you, thank you!

Aaron Olumuyiwa – My sweet son, I never fully understood a mother's love until you came into my life. You are such an inspiration to me and a constant reminder that I have to fulfil purpose. May you be a daring, shining light unto your generation.

Saidat Bolatumi Oloko – My dear mama, I will always be grateful to you for your guidance and sacrifices. You are easily the strongest woman I know (almost everyone says this about their mommas, but oh well!). Thank you, ma.

Adeola Oloko – Dad, thank you for everything you are to me. Life came with so many storms that threatened our relationship, but I'm thankful through it all.

My siblings – *Omotayo Harrison, Omolola Doris, Oreoluwa David, Oluwaseun Omotade*. Thank you for being my companions for life, thank you.

My niece and nephews – Oluwakanyinsola Dara, Jirola, Obaloluwa, Iremide, Omodesire, Ayotomiwa, Fikore, Noah, and the others to come. God bless you, my darlings. May you be a shining light to your generation.

My larger family members and friends –To my parents-in-law: the Olumuyiwas thank you for everything, I appreciate you. To all my sisters-in-law and brothers-in-law, thank you for everything that you are to me. To my church family and all my amazing friends who inspire me and never get tired of me, thank you for your support.

My publisher – A big thank you to Harmony Publishing who provided the management, editing and graphic designing services for this dream to come to life.

Contents

I

My Why

I recall one particular afternoon in late 2015 when I was sitting on a bed in an hotel where I'd been lodged by one of my office clients. I had a great job that took me all around the country. Being in my early twenties, I was a young, single, energetic female professional with no too many cares in the world. My life was not perfect but it wasn't spiralling beyond control either. I was focused and diligent at work, the darling of many. I knew God and I loved Him. I definitely wanted to serve Him more. Except I was always busy. The bulk of my time was spent reviewing clients' processes, preparing reports or traveling to a new city where my client was. By the end of the day, I was typically exhausted wanting only to relax and be taken care of – I deserved that.

I felt a need for me to be much more than just my consulting life, I just didn't know how to do that with such a demanding job. And it was a dream job in its own right; few years prior, I'd gone through the rigors of becoming a Chartered Accountant so I could land that kind of job and honestly, I'm ever thankful for that job. Yes, it was the kind of job that easily swallowed you up but I wouldn't dare complain. I considered myself very lucky to even have that job given the labor statistics in Nigeria at the time. There was just this one thing: I had a yearning to be much more than I already was, to do more. I was busy but unfulfilled. I had no spare time yet I was bored within me. Life was good but it felt like something was missing. There had to be more. I had one or two ideas that I thought God had placed in my heart or something, but where was the time to pursue them?

Then, it started. I picked up my laptop and began to type. I poured out the things that made my heart heavy and those that I sensed were laid on my heart. It was a Saturday and windows open, I glanced at the grey sky outside – it looked as burdened as I was. My heart seemed to hold a lot of content in it that day, and I didn't hold back. Poured it all out. After a couple of hours, it was in front of me. Not clearly but it was. Three typed pages filled with a ton of questions and convictions, something about finding my life's purpose. Why was I on earth? What was I created to do? What was my mission in this world?

This was it, the heavy burden that had been on my mind for God knows how long. How would I actively live my life in a way that would make a difference; a way that would make my heavenly father proud of me when I finally see Him face to face? It would take me a while to fully grasp the concept, and definitely a lifetime to live out my purpose. But alas I felt like I was onto something! And the first thing that was revealed to me in that moment was that if I was going to live a life of purpose, my life could NOT be about me. Huh?

That hunger that was impressed on my heart that weekend

remained there every day after that (some days, more prominent than others), it still is. It's like once that realization comes, you can never get rid of it no matter how much you try to suppress it. So, I decided to share what I had written to see if anyone else was thinking what I was thinking. I first shared it with my then fiancé, now husband. Then, I shared it with a few of my close work colleagues and friends. I remember thinking *Surely, I must not be the only one who is bothered (better still, confused) about this whole purpose thing, can we all just be confused together?* Most of them could relate. This stirred up some really interesting conversations among us as we attempted to unravel the mystery of life and its purpose.

How many times have you heard the word 'purpose'? Perhaps at a conference or from a friend or mentor. Or maybe you stumbled on it while reading a really good book. But how do we fully grasp this almost ambiguous concept? The truth is that it will take us a lifetime to do so. But I also think this makes sense, since purpose is the whole point of our lives. Purpose is about our lives bearing good fruits and doing what we're supposed to do on this earth. How do we know what we're supposed to do on this earth? By going back to the author of our lives. This means that ultimately, we can and will find guidance for our lives from the one who gave them to us. I'll try as much as possible to simplify things in this book with practical examples, some of which might sound a little cheesy like this one.

Automobiles and Grandma

One of the fastest cars in the world is the Hennessey Venom F5 and it can drive as fast as 301 miles per hour. The manufacturers of this car may have had a couple of things in mind when they created this automobile. But for all the possible reasons why this vehicle was made, it definitely could not have been made for the purpose of being stowed away in a garage its entire life. We can take a couple of guesses about what it was made for but the best way to know would be to just ask the vehicle's manufacturer; should save us a lot more time. That's step one and the most important step.

The second step would probably be to assess the vehicle's innate abilities. What do we know about this car? We know that it's been designed with high-speed functionalities. We also know what it's not - it definitely doesn't look like it was made to serve as a fertilizer spreader on a little country farm? Step two tells us that there are things we were created for and there are things we were not created for. But for us humans, we shouldn't skip step one before we get to step two.

Before today, some of us have been like the Hennessy Venom that never left the garage (fulfilling zero purpose) while some of us are at best being used as a fertilizer spreader (fulfilling the wrong purpose). Made for one thing, used for another. Let's take one more kindergarten example. Imagine you gifted your grandmother an iPad but she ended up using it to chop vegetables in her kitchen instead. She wasn't sure what to use it for and she didn't ask. It had a smooth surface so she figured it'd be a great substitute for her chopping board. No matter how much you tried to hide it, you'd be disappointed at how this gift you gave her was being used. The fact that it can be used for chopping vegetables doesn't mean that it should be used that way.

This is how it is when you and I do not live in the purpose for which we were created; when we don't realize that we were made for much more than just participating in life's rat race – be born, go to school, get a good job, get married, have kids, raise those kids and at 65, have a rethink about your entire existence (whatever that race looks like for you). And while all of these beautiful life events could be among God's plan for us, we should ensure that God is coming first in all our life steps, that if we're doing anything, it's because our will has aligned with His will for us, and we're not just following societal expectations. That per time, we're not just living for the next 'life milestone'. Fulfilling purpose may sound complicated, but it really wasn't designed to be. If we've never taken time out to discover what our purpose is, we'll never be able to live it. Purpose is a combination of who you are (read as: who God says you are and His calling on your life) and what you do with you are. And we'll discuss this in detail later.

This book is not a book of rules. It's a reminder that no matter how long we live, we have little time on our hands in this earth and we will give account of how we lived. A reminder that we are the light of the world, the salt of the earth, and that the world is waiting on us to manifest. That there are lives on the other side of our obedience. A reminder that we need to be good stewards of the gift that God has placed in our hands (think the iPad gift story from earlier) and that we need to bear good fruits.

My favourite part about writing this book is that as I

thought and typed out these words, I learnt a multitude of lessons myself – I can't begin to explain how much I have learnt and still am learning. I knew what I was going to write about from the start; what I didn't know was to what extent or level of detail I was going to go. I thought I knew what I was talking about until I began writing, listening, researching, and placing my understanding side by side with scriptures. Writing this book has opened me up to a whole new world of knowledge and understanding that I will never now take for granted. I can't believe I'd been sleeping on all that understanding and now I wish I had a loudspeaker to wake other people up. In the meantime, I'll just make do with this book as a proxy for my loudspeaker.

My prayer is that as you read on, you'll be fired up to live a life of purpose and intention, a life more than ordinary. I hope that this book spurs you to ask yourself those tough questions that'll help you find true meaning and clarity. I hope that it speaks to your soul and challenges you to stretch yourself beyond your limitations to ultimately be who God has called you to be. I hope that it causes you to want more of Him so you can know more of what He's deposited inside you. Enough of living in the fear of not knowing whether the Father will say to us 'Well done' when our time on earth is done.

II
So, Why Not?

"For we are God's handiwork, created in Christ Jesus to do good works, which God prepared in advance for us to do"

— Ephesians 2:10, NIV

I don't know how old you are right now but I want you to cast your mind back ten years ago. Where were you at that moment in your life? What were your dreams, your aspirations, your fears?

Okay, come back to this very moment and let's go over the following questions together:

- On a scale of 1-10, 1 being the lowest and 10 being the highest, how truly fulfilled are you?
- If you died tomorrow, will you be convinced that you were dying 'empty'?
- Are you living your life to the fullest of its potential?
- Do you know the purpose God created you for?

- Are you living out that purpose?

There are only a few things in this life that will stand the test of time and they will survive us after we are no more. The implication is that a good number of the things we are spending our time doing right now will not actually stand the test of time (and to some extent, this is inevitable because basic human activities like eating or playing don't need to stand the test of time). Question is, is there any portion of what you're currently doing with your life that you think can stand the test of time? I don't know about you but I don't want to be that person who just lived a 'basic' life. I don't want to be that person who had a 100% power voltage residing in them but only used up 5%.

The ones who will have truly lived at the end of their lives are the ones who fulfilled purpose while they were here. The ones whose positive impacts we felt the most. The ones whom we saw and felt God through. They are the ones who will have truly served others. The fun part? Whether you know it or not, you have a purpose for which you were created. Only, it's your responsibility to discover and fulfil that purpose. Have you as an individual ever given thought to understanding your own purpose or is it something you're expecting to hit you like a meteor someday?

Most Christians I know are interested in knowing and fulfilling God's purpose for their lives. They believe that God should have a say in what they do with their lives. And this is good because it is the starting point. The only problem is that a handful are not sure how to and they don't really take the time to find out what it is – this was me.

So, let's begin. How can we truly be more? how can we walk in the fullness of God's purpose for our lives? Purpose is not one single activity. It is everything that your life stands for from start to finish. Everything that you have experienced from your birth up till now has been moulding you for the fulfilment of God's purpose in your life. Purpose is what connects the dots of your life together. The life that will fulfil purpose is the life that yields to God daily and will be steered by Him even on the days that we fall short - and there will be days like that. It's only Him who makes the many pieces of our lives make sense. Indeed, He brings the extra to our ordinary.

Understanding Purpose

Before we dive deeper, here's a little checklist I think might help us understand some basics:

- Your purpose is found in God and is the very essence of your life.
- Put simply, your purpose and mine is to let our lives glorify God because He loved us first (see again the verse of scripture at the beginning of this chapter)
- Your purpose never changes but your assignments can change, depending on your season of life.
- Your purpose is not just about you. You understand that other people will be impacted by your decision to walk in purpose.
- Your purpose is what drives and motivates you in life.
- You feel a sense of fulfilment when you are living out

your purpose and maximizing the potential that God placed on the inside of you.

- Fulfilling purpose is a choice and it has to be done intentionally. You don't stumble on it by mistake and it can't be done for you (not even by Alexa or Siri).
- Once understood, purpose is the game changer, like a shining beacon in the dark.
- God's purpose for us is defined, it's not a mindless chase after the wind.
- Purpose is not driven by a hunger for pointless fame or wealth.

A few years ago, I was at a meeting when the guest speaker said: 'It is very sad that when some people die, many books will die with them.' And although books are figurative here, that statement hit me to my core. That day, I personally decided that I wasn't going to be one of those people who would die with all the potential God had deposited in their lives. I want to die empty and not full because what's the point if I go to the grave with every gift I was born with? God does not need us to come back to Him with the gifts and talents He gave us, there's plenty where those came from. We are to use it here on earth to fulfil His purpose.

Our Gifts; His Glory

Everyone has at least one assignment to fulfil in this world and it's our duty to understand what those assignments are. We have different capacities to handle various tasks and God knew what He was doing when He gave each of us our individual talents and assignments. So, if you ever wonder why some 'chosen few' seem to have more talents in their portfolio than you do, it's high time to understand that this isn't anyone's business to worry about and you too were made for more. I know it's easy to fall into the trap of: '*Oh the things I would achieve if only I was as talented as this other person.*' But I have also learnt not to compare my race with that of anyone else. The real food for thought should be: What am I doing with that little talent I've been given? Has it bloomed in my hands or am I going to return it to the giver the way it was given to me? Don't be that guy who went and buried his talent because it was 'insignificant' when he compared it to that of others. And you probably know the rest of that story.

When God is trying to send us on a mission, He'd typically place it on our hearts. If we are spiritually conscious enough, we may begin to develop keen interest in that particular area and find it hard to get it off our chests. Even if we're able to suppress that nudging briefly, we can be sure it'll find its way back one way or the other. A friend once said: if you can dream or envision something howbeit bigger than you it seems, it's probably because that dream is supposed to come to life. And I thought that was beautiful. The only thing I'd add here is that whatever dream or vision we believe God is giving us will always be in line with His word, and this is the best way to test those dreams and aspirations that we have.

Love is not forceful and because God is love, He will never force you to do anything that you don't want to do. He can and will walk you through those steps if you let Him but He won't take that actual step for you. He will reveal your assignment to you if you ask Him but don't expect Him to force you to move. Why? You get a say. You have a choice. He has given us free will, all of us.

He uses those who are willing so the question isn't about whether God will show you what He wants you to do; the question is whether you'll surrender and follow His leading when He does. Purpose is not only for a special set of people or your church ministers. If anything, you become a minister the moment you choose to align yourself with God's purpose for your life.

Seed-planting to Fruit-bearing

Why do farmers plant seed over their soil? They typically have an expectation that the seeds they have planted will germinate, sprout and bear fruits. In agriculture, the germination of a seed is majorly dependent on soil type, water availability, sunlight and temperature and when I can think of our lives, it's almost the same way. Soil type signifies how fertile our hearts and minds are to the things of our Lord. So, what kind of soil are you? Clay, sand or loam? Water: who or what are we allowing to water our lives? Are our lives being constantly nourished by rivers of living water or is our growth starved by the irrelevant things we absorb from social media, TV, and the world at large? Sunlight: are we still living in the dark like people who have not received the truth, or have we surrounded ourselves with the light and insight that comes only from above? Lastly, what's the climate and temperature of our lives? What's your spiritual, mental, and emotional state? At the end of the day, the point is that we get to decide whether we want to germinate and bear fruits or not.

God makes no mistakes and if He's given you any talent, it's because He knows that you have the capacity to let it shine. If God has placed something in your heart, it means you have a message to deliver to the world, and our world desperately needs it. Will you take up the responsibility of getting it out there?

Happiness or Joy?

If you ever needed a reason to fulfil purpose, just take a look at the broken world we live in. A world where joy, pure joy is scarce, where people have forgotten what joy is really like. Yes, people can feel an occasional sense of happiness but there is something greater than this and that is the joy of the Lord. Do you see how needy the world is of a message of hope and a sense of purpose? In need of people like you and me who have come to the realization that we have a need to fill in this world, people's whose strength comes from a place of light and godly understanding?

Happiness is momentary but joy is everlasting. Happiness is brought about by life pleasures like wealth, getting a new house, bagging an impressive degree, getting a promotion at work or going on a vacation; all of which are absolutely wonderful things in themselves. Who wouldn't want to have them? These things are awesome but they cannot give you joy in themselves. Joy is found when we're in Christ and we understand that we're here on a mission – a mission which certainly includes loving the Lord our God, loving people, and serving them with the gifts God has given us. This kind of joy and peace found in God are unlike the one that the world offers us.

In a generation where all sorts of information are at everyone's fingertips and young people look to the world to define what happiness is - only to be later disappointed, how do we make sure that the accurate message is out there? How do you and I encourage this generation and coming generations to understand that they have a choice and they don't have to look to the world to define who they are? By letting God's light shine through us no matter our walk of life. So, whether it's at your school, workplace, or business, you have the opportunity to spread the light of Jesus, and make positive impact. We were made for such a time as this, we were built for more.

Starting Where We Are

When should you start fulfilling purpose? Now. We humans like to wait for things to be perfect but there will never be a perfect time to start tapping into the 'more' that God has called us to be. Start where you are. Jim Elliott, the great missionary who became a martyr at age twenty-eight, said: '*Wherever you are, be all there*'. And indeed, it's as simple as that (note that I said simple, not easy). Because God is everywhere, we can to live for and with His glory wherever we are as long as we're now His. To live in the fullness of our potential, we need to have a yearning to lead lives dedicated to God. A thirst that can neither be created nor quenched by another human; a thirst to want to serve and be used by God. A thirst only His Holy Spirit can give.

The only way we can have this burning in our hearts is when we have a relationship with God and an understanding of how He wants us to live our lives. There is nothing as fulfilling as knowing what you were created for and living it daily, even if it comes with more work. At one of my past jobs, we had a common saying: '*the reward for hard-work is more work*' and I think that this obtains generally in life. God can entrust us with more when we've handled our little very well. And while it may seem so, this isn't a promise to have a more stressful life once we begin to go deeper with God. It's a promise for an effective life, a life that does more than ordinary, a life of impact.

Sometimes as we grow in life, we tend to try our hands in different things in an attempt to discover where our talents may be, like some sort of guess work. And while there is nothing wrong with self-discovery (I've done this a lot), nothing compares to having divine knowledge of where and how we're supposed to function. Let's normalize having conversations with God again, He still wants to speak to us. This can save us a lot of stress and time because then, we're able to channel our energy into a few relevant things rather than into every single thing there is. We must also bear in mind that even with God, life is not a straight-line movement so we better be ready for challenges. And can I encourage someone today, that while you're waiting on your a-ha moment, hold on to whatever honorable thing it is that you find yourself doing. Don't be idle in your waiting season – every season has a purpose. Living for God and fulfilling purpose is the journey of our entire lives and is filled with many discoveries and learning points. Only, we're not doing it all by or for ourselves.

For us to fulfil purpose and key into all that we've been made for, we've got to be intentional. Living intentionally comes from an awareness that we will one day give account of how we spent our lives. It is the act of saying and living: *'Lord, I recognise the fact that you gave me this life and I choose to honor you with it, teach me how you want me to do this.'* We reach our highest potential when we're fulfilling God's purpose. We become able to do much more beyond what our minds could have ever conceived.

The Author of Purpose

You probably already caught on this by now, but the starting point to fulfilling purpose is in realising that God is the author of purpose. This does not sound politically correct but it doesn't undermine the fact that it's the truth. We can come up with a ton of other ways or explanations but it's in Him alone that we can truly find ourselves. If it has to be done outside of the Lord, we're probably just doing our own thing (even if it's a good thing). Although they sometimes come together, being famous is not synonymous with fulfilling purpose, at all. And that's something we want to always keep in mind, especially because the world tries to tell us otherwise.

If God is the author of purpose, how then do we know what He wants us to do specifically? How do we know what His good and perfect will is for us? Here is an example of the kind of conversations/prayers I used to have with God whenever I wanted to 'know His will', especially those times when I needed to make major life decisions.

Me: Thank you Lord for the gift of life and I thank you for the grace to see this day. I'd really like to know what your will for me is in XXX area?

God: *Silence*

Me: You know, I really want to do your will but you gotta show me first, right? I mean, how can I do your will if you wouldn't tell me what it is?

God: *Silence*

Me: Are you even listening to me?

God: *Silence*

Me: There you go leaving me with the guess work again. Sigh. And then I leave feeling disappointed or even more confused.

Directly or indirectly, some of us have had these kinds of conversations with our heavenly Father. We try so hard to hear from Him and when we hear nothing, we start to wonder if He really does hear us when we pray, or if He really exists. We wonder if we can truly have that father-child relationship we were promised. Here's the good news: it's not even that complicated. What is the problem with the above conversation? Is it wrong to ask God what His will is for us? If we don't, how do we know if we should take that job? Or marry that person?

There is absolutely nothing wrong with asking God for what His will is on specific issues of life. In fact, it shows that we desire to do His will. Here's where the problem lies: He already gave us the answer to this question and many others thousands of years ago (although He could also speak to us audibly if He pleases, this doesn't happen very often). If I could take a wild guess, I would imagine Him rolling His eyes whenever we ask Him questions like this over and over again. Most of the time, the ready-made answer to many of the questions we ask Him is:

"...Seek ye first the kingdom of God and all these things shall be added unto you." - Matthew 6:33, KJV

In everything we're asking God for, we can always tell if the desire is coming out of a sincere love and hunger for Him or not. Will that thing we desire bring us closer to Him or draw us farther away from Him? In seeking Him, He reveals Himself more and more to us. In seeking Him, we get to know Him better. In seeking Him, we become more familiar with His ways and how He speaks to us personally. In seeking Him, we learn to love Him deeper. He isn't a genie who is just there to answer a yes or no question when we feel like asking Him, He wants a personal relationship with us. For every situation that we find ourselves in, for every decision that we need to make, our response has to be in line with the word of God. If it will take us away from His presence, it's not His will and purpose for us. This understanding is golden and it changed my life and relationship with God.

Who You Are Over What You Do

While it makes God glad when we do things that could potentially bring glory to Him, He is more interested in our 'being' than our 'doing'. He is more interested in who we are and in having a relationship with us, than in us trying to check some boxes of wanton achievements. We have to be close to Him before we can truly know His heart and do what He has called us to do. If we're so particular about *doing* while on the other hand neglecting our positioning in Christ, we're still missing the point. If I could summarize this section, I'd say purpose is: first, God loving us by paying the ultimate price for us, we reciprocating His love and learning to abide in His presence, then we loving and adding value to the people around us because of the previous two reasons. If you stopped reading this book at this point and take what you've gotten so far with you, I think I'll be good. Because then, you would have gotten a fair idea of what you need to know which serves as the foundation for the rest of this book. But of course, I wouldn't want you to stop reading now. We still have some important things to cover, so please stay with me (insert big smiley face).

Breaking down God's Purpose for Us

Every single person walking the face of this earth has a purpose to fulfil. The problem is that most people care less about anything that doesn't put food on their table. All children of God have a collective purpose irrespective of their color, race, age, height or weight. That purpose is the one of reconciling men back to God; the great commission. We have the responsibility of spreading Christ's redemptive message. We will not all go on mission trips but there are other ways we can do this in our daily lives. Our lives are living letters; speaking more than our words ever will.

Sometimes, I might even think of it like an employer–employee relationship. You have a brand you should ideally embody and reflect. When we become saved, we become representatives of God's kingdom here on earth. The only difference is that we're actual children of God and not just employees. So yes, let's all 'do our jobs' and promote the brand wherever we go. Don't keep the good news all to yourself. To be honest, I understand that it's becoming increasingly difficult to do this in our world today. I mean, who wants to be cancelled? Yet, it's important that we remind ourselves that this world is only temporary and not our final destination, or theirs. Real life begins at eternity and the choices we make here determine where we end up there.

Spreading the word is serious business for all children of God; a cause that regular people like you and me have lost their lives for. '*The cross before me, the world behind me*' were the last words of Nokseng, a man from a Meghalayan tribe in North-eastern India in then Assam, before he was executed. Nokseng along with his family had decided to follow Christ in the middle of the 19th century and clearly, this didn't go down well with those around him. Called to renounce his faith by the village chief, the convert declared: '*I have decided to follow Jesus.*' His two children were killed and in response to threats to his wife, he continued, '*Though no one join me, still I will follow.*' His wife was also killed before he was finally killed. If you think Nokseng's words sound like a popular hymn, you are correct. And while you might rightly think that what happened to him was the worst thing ever, listen to what happened next.

Nokseng's display of faith was reported to have led to the conversion of the same chief and village members. And although this won't change the fact that what happened is utterly saddening and barbaric, it wasn't for nothing. There are countless other stories like this, starting with the apostles we read about in the bible. So, when you and I take the great commission with levity, what we're inevitably saying is that we don't understand the gravity of the task that has been placed in our hands. We were never called to a life of convenience, nor were we placed on earth to be cute. The earlier we realize this, the better we're able to focus on the task ahead.

Individually-specific Assignments

Earlier, I mentioned that our purpose never changes but our assignments could change depending on many factors – and here's where we talk about that. To fulfil that purpose that we just talked about on the previous page, we are given individual assignments according to our gifts and talents, all of which should still point to that singular purpose somehow. Those individual assignments are the other component of fulfilling purpose and living extraordinary lives. We all have a specific part to play in God's purpose per time and this will tie back to our collective assignment because God will never contradict Himself. The remaining part of this book will speak more towards how we can be well positioned for these specific assignments.

Once again, our individually specific assignments cannot be in opposition to God's word and principles because God will never call us to something that He cannot control. He will not lead us into doing things that bring disrepute to Him. If it's not bringing glory to His name, it's not Him.

> *"For just as each of us has one body with many members, and these members do not all have the same function, so in Christ we, though many, form one body, and each member belongs to all the others. We have different gifts, according to the grace given to each of us"* - Romans 12: 4-6, NIV

What About Others?

Let's have this tough conversation really quick. What about people who don't believe in Christ? You may ask. Does this make them incapable of fulfilling purpose and living truly extraordinary lives? Could purpose mean different things to different people? These are valid questions and although they're difficult, we need to dive into them if we're going to fully grasp what true purpose is.

For starters, anyone can be wealthy or have a successful career in life, Christian or not. However, not everyone can truly fulfil purpose. From the beginning of time, God instituted a system by which the earth naturally operates. So, anyone who works hard has a potential to be successful in the same vein that people who have sexual intercourse have a potential to procreate. And this applies to everyone on the face of this earth regardless of their faith or beliefs - a natural order of life. I know Christians who while young were led to believe that you can't be wealthy unless you're a Christian and this is simply not true. Isn't it obvious? Then these ones grew up and realized they were lied to and they hold a grudge against the church and everything that accompanies it. So again, you don't have to be a Christian to make money or be 'successful'.

Now that we've established that, here's the difference for the believer in Christ: first of all, success is not what your life looks like compared to someone else's, success is what your life looks like compare to what God has in store for you as an individual. Success is how much in sync with the creator you are in your life. Secondly, aside from the promise of eternal life after we leave this world, God is interested and involved in everything that concerns us here on earth. This is the only reason we will be able to see His supernatural hand at work in the seemingly ordinary affairs of our lives. This is why things can happen to us that defy logic and reasoning, it is why favor can follow us wherever we go. Beyond a comfortable life here on earth though, He is absolutely more interested in the salvation of souls and our eternal fate.

And that is what defines purpose for us. Living with the understanding that there is something to come after this life. Living on earth as stewards who refuse to be distracted by everything going on in this world; who have the understanding that eternity is the goal. Regardless of the fact that more than half of the world's population may not believe this, we who have this understanding are to live our lives in line with it. It is the life we've been called to live.

Living the Good Life or Fulfilling Purpose

Let's look at this from another angle. According to the *Oxford Dictionary*, purpose is the reason for which something is created, made or done. The *Cambridge Dictionary* defines purpose as the reason why something exists or the reason you do something. *Collins English Dictionary* defines purpose as the reason for which something is made and done. I tend to like these – these folks get it. It's what we've been discussing all along; purpose is simply why we were created.

The above all seem to point to the fact that anyone's purpose is the reason they were created or born into this world. This means that it was by no mistake that you were born, even if you're a product of an unplanned pregnancy. God makes no mistakes; we humans are the ones who do. And if purpose is the reason why something was created, how wrong would it be to separate the purpose of a thing from its creator? For me, I think it will be an aberration for me to separate my life's purpose from the one who created me.

"For in Him all things were created, things in heaven and on earth, visible and invisible, whether thrones or dominions or rulers or authorities. All things were created through Him and for Him." - Colossians 1:16, NIV

Permit me to digress for a little bit so we can understand the concept of our birth into this world. Our parents may have been the vessel but they're not the creator of our lives. I have a son who spent ten or so months in my womb and whom I gave birth to in a lot of discomfort. Yet, I didn't give that little guy his life and neither did my husband. We were only the instruments that brought Him into his physical existence and who have a mandate to guide him in the right way as much as we can. And so, even if you did not physically bear your child, it doesn't make you any less of a parent or lessen the assignment you have over them. The scriptures say: *'I knew you before you were formed in your mother's womb.'* None of us can create a life no matter how that child gets into this world. Life only springs forth when God says so and we're here because God would have us be here.

So, back to the point I was making before the digression, there's a difference between living the good life and fulfilling purpose. This is why anyone can be the wealthiest, most charitable person that walked the face of the earth but still be unfulfilled. In the eyes of the world, they may appear fulfilled but that's not really the case. Many people just want to live the good life but there is something much more than just doing that.

To know the Lord is to love Him, not just His form or His acts but His being. To know Him is to relate with Him personally, not just talk about Him from head knowledge. To know Him is to serve Him, not out of unwilling obedience or eye service but because loving and serving Him is all we ever really want to do. If we're going to know Him, we're going to have to surrender our hearts and thoughts to Him because that's how we become more familiar with Him. Are you living on your own agenda or is your deepest desire to see Him glorified?

III

Discovering Your Assignment

"Whatever is true, whatever is noble, whatever is right, whatever is pure, whatever is lovely, whatever is admirable—if anything is excellent or praiseworthy—think about such things."

— Philippians 4:8, NIV

Now that we've established what the common (heavenly) goal is, let's talk about how to find our individual place in all of this huge mission. To discover our specific assignments on earth and be able to accomplish it, we need to be spiritually sensitive. Being spiritually sensitive means that we're aware of when the Holy Spirit will have us act on something. And the only way to be sensitive is to practise and learn constantly. Practising and learning refer to the same old thing we've heard as children of God; spending time in the place of prayers, meditating on the word, worship, and fellowship. It is to spend the time needed on the things that can strengthen our relationship with the Father.

Like we talked about earlier, the Lord might impress certain things upon our hearts or make us deeply passionate about some things (and let's not forget how these passions will need to always align with the word of God otherwise they're coming from elsewhere). These impressions are there for a reason whether for teaching us certain lessons or for preparing us for something greater. If there's something God is leading you to be passionate about, test that thought or vision with the word of God but don't you ignore it. Do something about it. I know, I know it doesn't seem like a perfect or refined idea but if it's a divine idea, be rest assured that there's something God wants to bring out of it. And God can lead us to do different things from a urge to attend a beneficial training, to starting a business, going to school, writing that song, writing that book, blog post, anything at all.

Him moving your heart in a particular direction and you being sensitive enough to receive that instruction are the major ingredients but that's not all. There's nothing like godly passion blended with diligence – oh what a potent combination, a force. Diligence is an expression of your intentionality. When you're diligent with what God has placed in your hands, you're invariably showing that you're ready to be that more that He intended for you to be; that you're ready to enter into fullness. If you're more than ten years old, you would have already figured by now that everything good requires effort, from getting good grades at school to reaching a height in your career, even to managing our human relationships adequately. Diligence is how godly passion becomes godly impact (read that again).

And we can't do this if all we want to do is stay in bed all day long.

There might also be times when we're called to an assignment that we ordinarily had no passion for (this can happen because serving God is much more than relying on our feeble human emotions). Moses protested that he was a man of slow speech. Jonah ran away, or so he thought, to where he ended up being swallowed by a fish before he was redirected to fulfil purpose. Jeremiah thought it appropriate to inform God that he did not know how to speak because he was too young.

Listen, it doesn't matter how imperfect or young you think you are. When God sends you on an assignment, it's because He knows that you can do it Him by your side. I understand that this isn't always an easy decision to make because it might require us to sacrifice a lot of our comfort and personal ambitions (whew). But there's no better decision than saying yes when He sends. I find that as time goes by and our understanding of God deepens, we begin to understand why we were chosen for that assignment.

Where to Fulfil Purpose

We can fulfil purpose wherever the tides and waves of life take us. You might be a leader, working professional, student, entrepreneur, husband, wife, single person, or stay-at-home parent and in that very role, God wants to use you. There is purpose in every season of our lives and we shouldn't minimize the worth that God has placed on us. No matter how insignificant you might feel in the grand scheme of things, you're not just another person walking the face of the earth. Everything that God has called you to be? Be it all, even in the corner of your small room. Knowing how much potential we carry, we need to develop on a constant basis, a habit of asking God what He'd have us do. And be ready to listen to Him speak through His word or any other way He chooses. And be prepared to do what He asks.

Many of us with regular jobs have a tendency to get complacent with our 'ministry' because we've become so comfortable with carrying out our routine tasks (I know I can be guilty of this). Could it be the lack of time or stress that come with those jobs that makes us worn out? Understandably so, but then again, I don't really want to get to heaven and realize that all I ever did while on earth was just make money or survive while neglecting all the ways I could have touched lives with my life. How is it possible to not get lost in a crazy work system when as believers, we're required to be excellent in all areas of our lives? We'll look at this in detail in a later chapter.

From this point on, I'd like to go into the practicality of how to actually walk the walk and not just talk the talk. Let's start with the following questions:

1. Is there a yearning in your heart to be or do more?

If there's something you should be doing that you're not yet doing, you might get a constant nudge in your heart that something is amiss. Perhaps you feel like there's got to be more to life (and that's because there is). You might also feel like there's a void in this world that you need to fill – almost as though

God needs your attention and time for something. Don't ignore this nudge, it can be the answer to the questions on your heart. It's a reminder that you have a supreme purpose to fulfil, a role to play in our crazy world. To fulfil purpose, there has to be an awareness of a need; a realization that there will be a void on earth if we don't take our place. If we find that a thought or an idea is being continually impressed on our hearts, possibly embedded with solutions to issues we see around us, we want to pay attention to such nudges.

We can either keep trying to figure life out on our own or we can decide to trust the one who has it all figured out already. The more we suppress that gentle voice of the Holy Spirit with worldly distractions, the less we hear it, only that doing so won't profit us. There are lives on the other side of our obedience and running away only leads us down the path of frustration.

I once read an article by a Brion Kallinen who knew as a teenager that he was called to full-time ministry (and this will be different for each believer) but decided to pursue his passion for truck-driving. He wrote: '*What I'm telling everyone who reads this is, if you feel God calling you to do something, it can be anything from becoming a pastor of a church or bringing an elderly neighbour a meal. Do it*'. Brion went on his way for about 30 years and after a number of failed businesses and marriages, he was back at the Father's feet where he should have never left. He's now using his story to encourage people about the pointlessness of running from God. Do you sense God leading you to something today?

2. What are your heart's desires and how does it align with God's word?

"For it is God who works in you to will and to act in order to fulfil His good purpose" - Philippians 2:13, NIV

What are your life's dreams? What does your heart hunger for? What legacy do you want to leave behind? How do these desires align with God's word? Anyone can have dreams and aspirations; my best guess is everyone probably does. What makes yours different as a child of God? Are your dreams inspired by God? Do those dreams have the potential of adding value to the lives of other people? One way to test if your dreams or desires are from God is if you have no idea how you'll achieve it especially in the beginning. No kidding. Most God inspired dreams are bigger than us. If it's easily achievable, it's probably a dream we can achieve by our own power. The world at large understands this concept too, hence the saying '*if your dreams don't scare you, they're not big enough.*'

Another way to test if your aspiration or dream is from God is that this big dream is probably doesn't revolve around you. It didn't spring out of a hunger to just become rich and famous and neither was it about you just marking items off your big-achievements register. God-birthed dreams come with an understanding that actual lives that will be transformed when that dream comes to life.

A third and most important check to know if your dream is from God is that it does not go against His word. I know I've said this a couple of times already but it's just so fundamental if we're going to sift our voice from God's. If our dream or desire is the kind that'll cause us to sin, we already have your answer. It doesn't even matter if 'everyone else does it'. He'll never modify His word to suit our conveniences and His word never returns to Him void because it will fulfil the purpose for which it was spoken. We can't have dreams that contradict His will as laid out in scriptures, and expect Him to validate them. We can't bribe or lobby God into our selfish desires.

Occasionally, God might confirm His will for us through a direct encounter with Him. Encounters could come in form of visions, dreams, trances, His audible voice or even words of knowledge (and these things can still happen today). Usually when these happen, they are hard to shake off and forget. And honestly, there's absolutely nothing in this world like having personal encounters with God. Encounters can happen to any believer, unbelievers even, like Saul of Tarsus later Apostle Paul who eventually wrote about thirteen books in the New Testament. God can reveal Himself to us in different ways as He pleases and when He does, we'll never be able to deny that He exists and has a specific plan for us. But we don't have to wait till He does, we already have all the direction we need in His word. We just have to spend more time in it.

"...By the mouth of two or three witnesses, every word shall be established" - 2 Corinthians 13:1, NLV

I just thought I'd add a final point here which is that sometimes God will reveal things about us to others – and no, it's not that God can't keep a secret. Part of me wonders if God resorts to this method when He's dealing with some of us who are doubting Thomases or when it's that we're just too far gone away from Him to hear Him directly or we're not yet familiar with how He speaks to us. Because really, some of us will see all the signs but still be in doubt or try to re-negotiate with God. And I think that for whatever reason, it's so easy (or convenient) for us to believe what another human says over what the Lord says. Whew, blessed indeed are those who believe without seeing. At the end of the day, nothing beats hearing God for and by yourself. All children of God have complete access and capacity to hear their Father. And while we might not all hear His voice audibly like Samuel did or speak with Him directly like Moses, this is why He gave us His Word and Holy Spirit to guide us through life. May we all be able to tap into these amazing resources at our disposal.

3. What's your why?

When I was applying to different schools for my MBA, I wrote a handful of essays like everyone else. You had to answer questions like why you wanted to go to graduate school, and what you hoped to get out of it. I wasn't used to doing stuff like this as it wasn't something I did before I got into my undergrad program back home. Yet, in doing this, I was learning an important lesson that eventually made me appreciate the essence of this requirement.

It helped me really think and ask myself why I wanted to go to graduate school and why I was applying to said schools. Was I just applying because people in my age bracket were doing the same thing? Was I applying because it seemed like the next smart move to make since my family had just relocated here? Was I applying because I just needed a good job? (honestly, this was like 80% of my reason at the time). So, whenever I was about to write my essays, I would take deep breath and try to calm those nerves. I would think deep about where I wanted to see myself in a number of years and how that specific program was going to help me get there. But to do that, I needed to first convince myself that I wasn't doing it 'just because'.

I think that this can be applied to life, how that we need to have these introspections from time to time. I am such a big fan of the quiet because I think that's where you can think well without distractions, and I am a big thinker. So, here's my introspection tip: find a quiet place, get a notepad and pen, and have your Bible close by too for when certain scriptures drop in your heart, and have enough time to do this. Cast your mind to your gifts and talents, your strengths and weaknesses. Where do you need God to move in your life? What have you done well in the past and how have you yielded to God in the past? What do you think is the next level God wants to take you right now? What step might He be asking you to take?

Take time to reflect on your why. Why do you do the things that you do? Do you do things because you want to be popular or do you do things because you want to be a blessing to people? Intentions and motives are as important as the dream. Meditate on higher goals and on things above. Is your heart beating for the things the father's heart is beating for? Are you concerned about the things of God or are you just doing life on your own terms anyway? One of my life principles is: if it's not what God wants for me, I don't want it to be in my desires.

Are you just trying to prove people wrong or are you doing things with meaning and purpose? Don't get caught up in trying to prove to people that you're worth more than they think you are. Why not? Surely, this could this drive us to do big things, not so? Yes, but while this is true, our motives would be flawed since we might be doing those things out of bitterness or rage. I get it, we've probably all been there or close - people hurt us or look down on us, and then we vow to surprise them by proving them wrong with our last drop of blood. It's better for us instead to keep our eyes on God and protect our joy. It's quite refreshing to know that where the Lord is taking us, no one can stop us from getting there.

4. What are your passions and hobbies?

I know this one sounds a little basic but we need to understand what our passions and hobbies are so we can place them side by side with the word of God and know which to pursue and which are at best inspired by our flesh. The things we naturally excel at could be pointers to our specific assignments. Our competencies have a way of reflecting our individual assignments and how these fit into God's supreme purpose. We have our talents and skills for a reason - the fact that they help us function where we're called. When we know where we should be and what we're supposed to be doing, it's easier for us to fit into the puzzle.

> *"If your gift is to encourage others, be encouraging. If it is giving, give generously. If God has given you leadership ability, take the responsibility seriously. And if you have a gift for showing kindness to others, do it gladly." - Romans 12:8, NLT*

One person might have the gift of singing while another might be a dexterous artist. One an excellent counsellor - another, an astounding writer. Some might even be gifted with more than one thing and this is altogether wonderful. God is intentional about the gifts and talents that He gave us. Tip: Talent alone will not keep us where God wants us to be. Everyone can be talented but the best blend is when we combine our talent with diligence, skill and consistency.

5. What do other people think of you?

Contrary to popular opinion, it matters what other people think about you as a child of God. If it did not, the word of God would not refer to our lives as written letters for which people are to read, infer, and learn. In her book *How the World Sees You*, Sally Hogshead writes: *'It is not enough to think something of yourself, it's also important to know how you are viewed by the world.'* Perception is not the most important thing we need to fulfil purpose and step into the fullness of our potential but there is a place for it.

> *When Jesus came to the region of Caesarea Philippi, he asked his disciples, "Who do people say the Son of Man is?" - Matthew 16:13, NIV*

You know who you are? Great. You know who God says you are? Even better. But who do people say that you are? A question that Jesus Himself asked His disciples when He was physically here on earth. So, who are we not to? And I get it - we live in a world of 'do you, the world will adjust'. I don't even know who coined that but as Christians, we're not called to live a life of 'doing you'. This is important to consider because if we're talking about how we can positively impact people's lives, we probably shouldn't ignore their opinion of us. If the world sees us in a way that we believe is mistaken, we might have either sent out wrong signals about our identity or we've been truly misunderstood.

What do your colleagues at work think of you? Perhaps you're the head of your department but people keep saying that you're insensitive to the plights of your colleagues. Are they really all just wrong? Or your bosses and peers at work think you're lazy and ineffective. Is it really all just baseless rumour mongering? Occasionally, one or more people really could misunderstand us but if everyone's in sync about your personality, it's probably worth thinking about (especially when negative). Here's a more interesting angle: What do the people closest to you think of you? Who does your spouse or parent think you are when no one is watching? What do they think are your strengths and weaknesses? What do they think are your talents? The people closest to you are usually able to help identify your strengths and weaknesses. And although this may not always be the case, what they think about us could sometimes be the reminder that God has a special assignment for us.

What next?

Hopefully, the above questions stirred up some thoughts in you by now, but I thought I'd leave the following tips here to round off this chapter:

1. **<u>Put Your Hands to The Plough and Start Serving</u>**.
    As willing vessels, we have to demonstrate that we're
    ready to be used. Those things that come to us easily:
    our gifts and talents are usually the best place to begin
    serving. How can you use your talents to add value
    to other people, to bless lives? And although it's best
    to begin serving in those areas that come to us easily,
    we will need to do some difficult things at some point
    because it's also important that we grow. How can you
    use your gifts to start serving others today? How can
    you add value to your talents today?

    Along with my singing and writing, I've been want-
    ing to learn how to play a musical instrument for years
    now, mostly in my head. About ten years ago, it was
    going to be either the keyboard or guitar but recently,
    I told my husband it was now the violin. Talk is cheap
    though because as of the time this book was published,
    I still couldn't play any instrument. Perhaps if I'd been
    serious about learning since the first time, I would have
    been able to play one instrument now. As do many oth-
    er things in life, learning musical instruments take time
    and commitment, which I've not been able to gather
    yet. But the thing is I'll never know if I can do it well
    or not if I never try. What is it that you've been putting
    off trying?

2. **<u>Be open to learning</u>**. Are we learning from our mistakes
    and the things that happening in our everyday life? Are
    we learning from others? Are we seeking knowledge?
    This applies to every area of our lives: our relationship

with God, working through the assignments He placed in our hands, our relationship with family and friends, our careers, our businesses. Learning is a continuous process in life, it should never stop. If we ever wondered how certain people just do some things effortlessly, it's not that they didn't actually put any effort into it (I can't begin to explain to you how hard it was to put this book together.) It's just that they went through a refining process that got them to the desired result; they learned, unlearned, and re-learned.

3. **<u>Serve, serve, and serve again.</u>** Okay I know, this sounds like a repetition but I can't over-emphasize this. You will likely not be able to fulfil purpose if you don't embrace serving other people. It almost sounds demeaning but it isn't! It actually takes strength, love, and understanding to serve people who have nothing to give you in return. Take a look at Matthew 23:11: *'The greatest among you must be a servant' (NLT)*. I once gave an exhortation in a small women's group about how serving within a team - especially in God's household is one of the easiest ways to discover our God-given talents and this always rings true for me. Some of the best memories I have of discovering my God-given gifts are from my experiences in university when I served under my campus fellowship. If you can serve together with a team consisting of other people who also have a passion to fulfil God's purpose, even better because then everyone is working to achieve a unanimous goal, and everyone can begin to understand which part of the body they fit. No, you were not saved or called to

be a benchwarmer. So, serve in church, volunteer on that charity group, serve in your neighborhood, help someone without expecting anything in return. Let's get moving and serve. And when we're done serving, let's serve again!

4. **<u>Practice and be diligent.</u>** Naturally, the more we do something, the better we get at it. Let's not expect to be where we want to be from day one. There's a reason why it's a process. That process is what makes us become who God is calling us to be. All good things take time and some of the virtues we'll be needing on our way are patience and diligence. Diligence is how talent becomes impact. If we're not willing to be diligent in the things of God, we might as well not bother. Whatever the Lord has placed in your hands, be diligent at it and watch Him make all things beautiful in His time (not yours).

IV

Strength for The Work Ahead

"Now may the God of peace ... equip you with everything good for doing his will, and may he work in us what is pleasing to him, through Jesus Christ, to whom be glory for ever and ever. Amen."

— Hebrews 13:20-21, NIV

One of the key points I hope I will have made by the end of this chapter is the fact that it's important for us to surround ourselves with people who have a desire to be all that they were called to be; a desire to fulfil purpose as understood in Christ. Call it a support system, tribe, or community and you'd be right. The benefits of having a godly tribe are plenty and we'll be taking a look at these later. I come from an amazing family but I wasn't raised a Christian - so once I became born again, the importance of godly community became clearer to me.

Sometimes, I get a sense that people want to postpone doing God's will till later. If fulfilling purpose means taking one step closer towards God each day, why as children of God would we want to delay that? Why would we rather not live our lives in full service to God from the moment we become enlightened? And I believe the issue here is that it is indeed scary for us to relinquish the control of our lives to someone else - even when this someone is bigger than our minds can comprehend.

While it's best to jump on the *Built for More* life as early as we can in life, it's also okay if you find that you're late to the party (in case you're wondering why you're just finding out about all of this good stuff now). The most important thing is to begin to act on everything that you now know. I just felt a need to say that since one of the lies the devil tries to sell people is that they are too old to be used by God, too old to serve, or too old to fulfil God's purpose for their lives, too old to do and be more. But I have good news: it doesn't matter how old you are, how much money you have or how much troubles you've been through. I couldn't tell you how much it blows my mind every time I see how God uses the mess in people's lives for His glory.

Now, let's dive into how we can find strength for the work ahead because becoming built for more is no child's play:

1. Have a relationship with the author of purpose

I've probably said this in every chapter already but it remains the most important part of living out our purpose. If we don't know the Lord personally, we cannot understand the fact that He is the author of our lives and lives' purpose. My prayer is that every person reading this book will truly come to know Him and not just know of Him. And in order to have a relationship with God, we will have to first recognize and accept His love.

"For God so loved the world that he gave his one and only Son, that whoever believes in him shall not perish but have eternal life." - John 3:16, NIV

You think you love yourself, your spouse, and your kids? Well, God loves us and them more than we do. The human mind has tried to comprehend this love severally and for some, it's definitely some cock and bull story. But we serve a God whose ways are not our ways, and whom we could never fully comprehend. This is why He is who He is: God. If He allowed us to completely grasp Him, He wouldn't be God and there would be no need for faith. All of that to say: it's okay to have questions (we all should, even) but I have seen and experienced too much to deny the truth of God's love. If you haven't made Jesus Christ the Lord of your life, today is the day that you need to make that decision or re-dedicate your life to Him as the case may be. Being one with God, He is the author of purpose and without Him, we're just doing our own thing – no matter how nice we are or how much we donate to charity.

"For everything, absolutely everything, above and below, visible and invisible, rank after rank after rank of angels - everything got started in Him and finds its purpose in Him" - Colossians 1:16, MSG

As we begin to actively cultivate a relationship with God, we find that it is in Him alone that we can find and fulfil purpose. It is only with this understanding that we will not sink in complete frustration when (not 'if') things are not going smoothly in life. I think it's pretty obvious that if we're living our lives for money, fame, or other personal gains, life can quickly become frustrating when things don't go as planned. And the reason is because ephemeral begets ephemeral.

2. Stay connected to the source

> *"I am the vine; you are the branches. If you remain in me and I in you, you will bear much fruit; apart from me you can do nothing. If you do not remain in me, you are like a branch that is thrown away and withers; such branches are picked up, thrown into the fire and burned" - John 15:5-6, NIV*

It's not enough to realise that our purpose begins and ends with God and just leave it at that. Now that we know, what are we going to do about it? Many of us have had plumbing issues at some point in our adult lives – very quickly, let's consider whether a tap/faucet could ever bring forth water if it was detached from the water source. When I think of this, two scenarios come to my mind. The first is how irregular and all-over-the-place the water flow gets once the faucet is **somewhat** disconnected from the body although there's still some water flow. Doesn't sound cute but the second is equally bad if not worse: when the faucet is **completely** disconnected from the main water source or the water pipe is not at all connected to an aquifer. The result? No flow at all.

Let's think of God as the water source; we the faucet and the water that flows from our individual faucets/taps, our results and fruits. Are you bearing fruits? If so, what fruits are you bearing and how are you bearing them? What is flowing out of you? Does God flow out of you or does the world flow out of you? Is your water flow irregular? In God today, out tomorrow?

When we are completely disconnected from our source, we are that faucet that isn't bringing forth water and is really of no use. On the other hand, some of us are not completely disconnected from Him, it's just that we find it hard to maintain consistency in our walk with Him - finding it hard to get it together and ending up with a broken-pipe relationship with God. And the result is irregular or little flow of water. Why settle for broken when we can have complete? With God, we're either all in or out. Let us endeavor to not just go all in but stay in. Being all in definitely doesn't mean that we will not have challenges along the way, it just means that even then, we can be sure that God is with us and our spirit-man is still in sync with the master.

> *"Fixing our eyes on Jesus, the author and perfecter of faith, who for the joy set before Him endured the cross, despising the shame, and has sat down at the right hand of the throne of God" - Hebrews 12:2, NASB*

When I was preparing for my first road driving test, I quickly learnt the principle of *'where your gaze is, there your vehicle goes'*. This simply means that the direction we fix our gaze as we drive, is where our vehicle is steered by default. As a consequence, this means that whenever we're driving, we ought to keep our eyes where we want our vehicle to go – forward. Imagine if you fixed your gaze on the side curb or you let every and any distraction take your eyes off the road. All of this to say, let Christ have your attention and your life will naturally steer towards Him.

The way we can be truly fruitful and fulfilled is by staying connected to Him. This is especially true because when God has His eyes on us, we can be sure that the devil does too. As a result, he (the devil) will bring things right under our nose that will be an appearance of the real thing. Things to distract and derail us. But Jesus, He is the real deal. We find clarity and joy in Him - we find our purpose in Him. The Lord does not need us to be perfect, He only needs us to make a personal choice to submit to Him daily, walking with Him one day at a time. Let's stop doing life on our own because we think we have control over some things or small money (insert eye-rolling emoji); let's allow the Father walk us through life the way that only He can.

Disconnected without knowing it

Can there be times when we become disconnected from God without even realizing it? Yes. As stated above, this can happen when we're distracted by a ton of things or when we've just grown spiritually insensitive. I know we talked about the importance of serving in the previous chapter but don't get so busy serving others that your relationship with God suffers.

Let's learn to take time out to just be with and bask in the presence of our heavenly father. When He called us to our assignments, the intention was never for us to draw away from Him.

Speaking engagements, preaching invites, TV shows, book-writing, organizing music concerts, being a great employer or employee, being a parent or spouse, or whatever else we believe God called us to, are all great. But those things are not to become our god. Don't get so carried away with your calling that it draws you away from your actual relationship with God. Hey Abimbola, isn't that why you wrote this book? For us to become partners with God and fulfil purpose in the many areas of our lives? Absolutely. God loves it when we work for Him and partner with Him but more importantly, He wants us to have a personal relationship with Him.

> *"Martha, Martha," the Lord answered, "you are worried and upset about many things, but few things are needed— or indeed only one. Mary has chosen what is better, and it will not be taken away from her. - Luke 10:41-42, NIV*

If we continue to do "God's work" without the presence of His Holy Spirit, it's only a matter of time before it becomes obvious that we're running on *spiritual empty*. So, if you're doing what God called you to do and you notice that that business is putting a strain on your relationship with Him, go back to Him. Know when to take a break, slow down, and re-align your focus where it should be. If He brought you to it, only He can see you through it.

How then do we maintain the connection to our source?

There's no magic about it. It is by spending time with God through the study of scriptures, prayers, worship, and fellowshipping with other believers. All of these are integral to our faith walk. And I dare say that there's absolutely nothing wrong with getting creative in how you spend time with God. So go ahead, take that fun online bible quiz, watch that Christian movie, bask in Christian music, pause to pray in the middle of your day: these are ways that we can spice up our relationship with God in this day and age. Spending time with Him constantly is how we learn to recognise His voice and walk in obedience to Him. It is the way we know when He's speaking to us. When last did we sense God speaking to us or do we just reel out a list of prayer requests when we pray? Do we ever just stay still and listen to His voice? In his book, *A Praying Life,* Paul E. Miller talks about how we can over-spiritualize prayer or even fall into the trap of using a mechanical prayer 'system'. Is our prayer life a two-way communication street or is it one-way?

The great thing is that God speaks to us with everything around us, not only when we're actively praying. He is in the swift wind, nature, the people around us, indeed He is in the very air that we breathe. The ability to see God in everything around us is so liberating and by this, we develop spiritual consciousness. When we pray, we need to ensure open channels of communication both to transmit from our hearts and to receive from the heart of the Father. In our human relationships, we are told that communication should be two-way right? Fun fact: the same goes for our relationship with God.

I know there are times when we have a ton of requests and all we want to do is ask God for answers and a couple 'Yes-es' here and there. But there are different reasons why a prayer may 'seem' to not have been answered by God or the answer delayed. God is not punitive; He knows the concerns of our hearts and He isn't trying to make us suffer. But we need to remind ourselves that He wants the best for us and if He says 'No' to a request, it's because a 'Yes' would not be in our best interest.

Even when it seems otherwise, everything works out for the good of those who love the Lord and are called according to His purpose: you and I. It doesn't matter how difficult life is right now, He sees you, He knows your pain, He knows where the shoes hurt you the most. It may not feel like it right now but He does. (Side-note: I re-read this paragraph two-years after I wrote it and when I happened to be in one of those rough seasons, and I'm going *whew okay Lord!* So honestly, I know life can get pretty messy).

But really, sometimes, the answer to our prayer is in the strength that God gives us to weather the storm and not in the storm going away. Sometimes too, we're the ones delaying the answer to a prayer by not acting when He asks us to do. All of these is why we need to practice listening and hearing God to improve our spiritual sensitivity – so then, we can differentiate thoughts that come from God from the ones that come from our minds versus those that come from the devil.

"Dear friends, do not believe every spirit, but test the spirits to see whether they are from God, because many false prophets have gone out into the world." - 1 John 4:1, NIV

3. Be determined

Determination is firmness of purpose; the act of being resolute towards achieving something. And by now we already know what we should be striving to achieve: a life that seeks to please God, going where He sends, and generally building up ourselves for more of what He has for us. Determination is how you respond when you're not letting anything or anyone stop you from what God has in store for you. Determination is the spirit of not wavering in God even when we face obstacles in life.

Determination is the strength of our resolve to do the work God has called us to do. It is the decision to not give up on fulfilling God's purpose here on earth. Fulfilling purpose is no easy feat or a walk in the park; it indeed takes a great deal of determination, intentionality, diligence and spiritual sensitivity. I honestly think it's much more difficult to fulfil purpose than to be successful by worldly standards – because when we're in God, we also have to die to our flesh daily and be watchful of our motives.

I had a million and one reasons to never write this book or even finish it – just thinking about it all again makes me weak. I went on a hiatus at some point, almost quit at another, it was just too much for me given the fact that I had to combine this with the many other things in my life including nursing a baby at some point, relocating, going back to grad school, being a wife, mom, and honestly, just existing. I remember whenever the writing process got stressful, I would think: it costs a lot to put a good book out there, do I really have to publish this book? Where am I going to get all that money from? Why am

I having sleepless nights over a book that probably only a few people will read (because my goodness, the children of this generation no longer read!) or that'll only change one person's life? And that's the point. Even if it only changes one person's life, if the sleepless nights were because of that one person that'd pick this up and find meaning for their life, it was worth it. I can have questions, but it's not my job to focus on the many whys and limitations, rather it is to focus on the task I've been given.

Determination does not ignore the fact that there'll be rough patches on our way. Rather, it reminds us of why we started in the first place and gives us reasons to go on. What is that assignment that the Lord has given you? I know it seems hard to accomplish but if He gave it to you, best believe He wasn't trying to set you up for failure -it's because He knew you could do it. Without the help of the Holy Spirit coupled with our willingness and determination, I don't know how we could ever complete the assignments God has for us. But when we stick with God, the Holy Spirit will continue to give us those gentle nudges and reminders that we so direly need. Which brings me to my next point.

4. The Holy Spirit; our companion

Most of the remarkable things I've achieved happened when I listened to the gentle voice of the Holy Spirit (remember those subtle nudges we talked about earlier?). For me, this is a reminder that I have to continuously train myself to be spiritually sensitive because I, just like most people, can get carried away with the affairs of life (and I don't know about you but the affairs of my life are plenty). How sensitive are you to the things of the Spirit? Are you careful enough to be listening for when He speaks? Do you recognise how and when God speaks to you? Can you differentiate the many voices in your head from that of the Holy Spirit? The only way that we learn to recognize God's voice is by practice. Yes, practising to hear for that beautiful voice of God. Never forceful, only persuasive. Never aggressive, only convincing. Ever gentle, ever re-assuring. When He speaks, we who claim to be His children should be able to discern that it's Him. Sometimes, I miss it but I intend to keep practising, to keep trying.

> *"My sheep hear My voice, and I know them, and they follow Me. ²⁸ And I give them eternal life, and they shall never perish; neither shall anyone snatch them out of My hand." - John 10:27-28, NKJV*

5. Identify your unique qualities

Ever wondered why some people are outgoing or extroverted while others are reserved or introverted? Wherever you fall on the spectrum of personality type, you probably know how much of a struggle it is for you to try to be the other personality type. Although I think that we must find a way to strike a fair balance in our personality traits (there's no excuse for bad behaviour regardless of your personality type), I also believe that God designed us whichever way we are for a reason. You are not an extrovert or introvert by mistake. God needs your extroverted or introverted self to fill a need somewhere. A couple of years back, I took the Myers-Briggs test (an introspective self-report questionnaire which attempts to indicate various personality types based on your answers) for the fun of it, and the test speculated on my strengths and weaknesses which I'd say to a reasonable extent were accurate. I was almost like: is someone monitoring my life?

But beyond random personality tests like this, do we really know our identity? Who we are and what we stand for? What makes us tick? Our strengths and weaknesses? Most important-ly, do we know who God says we are? Because if we don't know who we are, the world will define it for us. Our strengths are pointers to those aspects of our lives we need to leverage on while our weaknesses are areas we either need to work on, or allow somebody else complement us in (surprise! you're not supposed to be good at everything). But that will only happen if we're able to identify these in the first place. What are your outstanding qualities? Could it be that God put those qualities in you for a reason?

6. Set godly goals

When I began writing this book, I didn't exactly start out with a time goal in mind. This in turn led to some time wastage and perhaps, I might have been able to complete it earlier than I did. But the moment I realized that it was an assignment big-ger than me and set a target, I became more dedicated to the work. I myself was amazed at the extents to which I went to ensure that those targets were met. This was possible because, now I had something I was running towards. Again, we should however always strive to make sure we are aligned with God's plan for us and not just pursue the goals that look pretty to us.

When we have a task - and it could be anywhere from simple to complicated such as lending a helping hand, bringing a smile to someone's face, preaching in a far-away nation, or just excelling at our work, it's probably in our best interest to consider how and when we want to achieve it. Maybe I'm more convinced of this because as a finance professional, goal-setting is not exactly negotiable for me. But I can't help but feel like this is applicable to all areas of our lives: from our jobs, to our relationship with God, friends and family, our ministry, and just living.

I find that it's helpful to set both short-term and long-term goals: short-term goals can span a period of hours, days, or weeks while long term goals can span months or years. Regardless of the nature of that goal, dare I say that we should do whatever we can TODAY; I mean, who promised us tomorrow? Goal-setting should not be an excuse to procrastinate since today may very well be our last on earth (and I don't mean to hurt your feelings when I say that – it's just fact).

> *Now listen, you who say, "Today or tomorrow we will go to this or that city, spend a year there, carry on business and make money. Why, you do not even know what will happen tomorrow. What is your life? You are a mist that appears for a little while and then vanishes. Instead, you ought to say, If it is the Lord's will, we will live and do this or that." - James 5:13-15, NIV*

Having established that, I find that although it's super easy to set goals in our minds, it's always better to have something documented that can be reviewed from time to time. And when we document it in a writing pad or whatever else, it's not to be shoved in the old travelling box in our garage. It should be in a place that is easily accessible for us to review and monitor. I like to use sticky notes in addition to my journal so I can have those goals staring me in the face when I wake up. You've probably heard that your goals should be specific, measurable, achievable, relevant and time-bound (SMART) and while this is an awesome way to think about goals (I use this almost all the time), I say don't waste time trying to come up with a goal that is SMART from the scratch. The starting point should be the goal, and then you can work your way back to making it SMART - and not the other way round, hopefully that makes sense.

That being said, let's get a little in the weeds of what a SMART goal might look like. How might we make a habit of setting achievable goals with achievable timelines in our daily life? If you are in business, let your client or customer know when the most realistic date for you to deliver your side of the bargain is. It's the right thing, the Christian thing to do. Don't lie to them because you want them to stay or because you don't want to lose that potential revenue to your competitor; they'll eventually leave when they realize that you disappointed them when that whole dishonest situation could have been avoided. I always appreciate and respect people who are truthful and honest from the start, and I'm sure most people do too.

Oh wait, an hilarious example just came to mind here and I'm sure you can relate if you've lived in Nigeria long enough. Many people in Nigeria like to have bespoke outfits made for them by fashion designers, particularly those made from those unique fabric prints - it's kind of just part of the culture. But there used to be this common joke about Nigerian fashion designers (or should I say, tailors?) and how some of them will promise to deliver your well knitted attire on a particular date but fail to deliver most of the time. Typically, by the time you're back to get your outfit, they may not have even touched your fabric at all, let alone start to work on it. I definitely had a few nerve-wracking experiences myself.

Imagine that you'd planned to wear said outfit for a friend's wedding (it's mostly weddings, don't ask, we just love weddings!) and your tailor/fashion designer having given you their word earlier delivers to you nothing but a 'I'm sorry, your outfit isn't ready yet' the evening before the wedding. No early notifications that they cannot meet up, just failed promises due to unrealistic goals that they set on their part. This is how your goals could affect the people around you, especially if you have a job or run a business. The above story is more likely to occur towards the end of the year because understandably, it just so happens that there's more customer traffic at that period. Most designers are already nearing their full capacity for the year by then, but some will continue to take on additional jobs regardless. Which in turn leads to customer frustration and overall loss of that customer. In whatever capacity we function in life, let's not be that person.

That being said, there are times when unforeseen circumstances will occur and this might influence some of our timelines and goals. And when this happens, what we need to do is duly modify those timelines and promptly inform those who are affected by that change - be it a boss, colleague, client, family member or friend. There are also times when we honestly need to update our goals as we become wiser, or more knowledgeable in Christ. When this happens, it's in our best interest to embrace necessary changes as the will of God supersedes all human plans and goals.

Once we've set our goals for a particular period, it might be helpful to share those with an accountability partner which we'll talk about in detail soon. This person's role is to follow up with you and periodically remind you of your goals and assignments, should you ever forget.

7. Have a strategy

Reflecting on what we've talked about so far, the order is: Accept Christ into your life, have a relationship with Him, find ways you can serve with the gifts He has given you, and set defined goals around this. The next step I'd like to introduce is: develop a strategy for achieving those goals. This doesn't mean that you're taking your life into your own hands. What it means when used in the right context is that you're being a good steward of the time and ideas God has given you. He gives us grace to be able to do the things He has called us to do but this grace will only apply when we learn to be good stewards. One of the ways we can do this is by adding value to ourselves and the gifts He has given us (remember again the biblical parable of talents).

A strategy is a plan - the how. God can give you the idea but He won't do the work for you. So, you know what He wants you to do but how do you intend to do it? How do you intend to step into the 'more' that he has for you? What are those practical steps you intend to take to ensure that you're in sync with God? How do you intend to live that life of positive impact He has called you to live? Who are the kinds of people you need to surround yourself with in order to be able to do this? We don't have to have the perfect picture (we never will); only a plan that reflects that we're really interested in living that life God has called us to live. This is what a plan or strategy does: helps us to have the mindset of a doer, and not just a hearer. Please know that a gift or talent not groomed can be lost or at best become ineffective.

Things may not always go the way we planned them even if we prayed while doing so. But because the bible tells us that all things work together for the good of those who love God, even then, things are still going according to plan. His plan! You may ask why then we should bother making plans? Because this can keep us from getting distracted and help us stay disciplined to the course God has laid in our hearts. Ultimately, our heart's posture when we make plans should be one of: *"Lord, I'm making this plan because it I believe it is honorable and is your will for me. But I also know that even if it doesn't work out, you have something better in store for me."* So go on, get your journal and pen, write out a quick plan for those things you believe God is placing on your heart to do, then say the above prayer again.

"For I know the plans I have for you," declares the Lord, "plans to prosper you and not to harm you, plans to give you hope and a future." - Jeremiah 29:11, NIV

8. Have a purpose accountability partner

Back to this topic of having an accountability partner. Your purpose accountability partner should be someone who knows and loves the Lord, someone who understands the importance of living a life of purpose. Someone who is excited to see you live in the fullness of all that God has for you. This person should be someone with whom you can discuss the challenges you're facing along the way. There will be days when what we just need is someone who can nudge us on in the middle of the challenges we face. This person can be there to encourage us to remain consistent in the Lord and remember what we've been called to do.

You also could in turn be a purpose accountability partner for somebody else; remember we not only want to receive but also give, and you could even be part of an accountability group where a few people come together to keep one another accountable for the assignments they believe God is calling them to do. It doesn't matter if we call them accountability partners, they could be our close friends whom we have such conversations with. Honestly, you could use any godly person in your life: mentor, spouse, sibling, parent, or friend.

It's important to note that our accountability partners are not responsible for how we live our lives; we are solely responsible for this. They might be able to keep us in check but at the end of the day, it's still up to us.

9. Do your homework

I personally find it soothing to research and dig up knowledge so by the time I started writing this book, I'd done a little homework and this habit never stopped till the book was done-done. Being my first book, there was just so much I didn't know about writing a book especially given the peculiarity of this book. I knew it was going to be a big learning process for me, and boy, what a whole school it was. I believe that for every idea that God gives us, He also graces us the capacity to bring it to fruition when we do our part.

If the Lord has led you to do something, I think it might help to know if there's anything out there that could provide insight for you. For example, to know if someone else has walked in your shoes before - to know the barriers they encountered along the way and learn from their experiences. It could be a deeper search into scriptures, godly books or related materials, it could be talking with people who have towed those lines before. Researching is such an effective learning tool and many times, a pointer to whether we are growing or not.

It's usually not hard to tell if someone is a good bible student because they have a desire to learn more about the word of God. Whether it's in researching about the meaning of *Leviathan* or learning more about the state of the Roman Empire in the day of the apostles, there's just that interest to know more. Let's not be afraid of asking the relevant whys. God is not intimidated by our questions! Some of us are afraid of researching into what we believe for fear that it might shake our belief system as though we're trying to 'protect God' from the unknown. Are your sources reliable? Definitely don't just gobble up everything you see on the internet. Do you have a witness in your spirit that you're not searching wrong or misleading material? Have other bible students used that source? Then, go ahead and learn!

Let me quickly share a laughable inside story, howbeit with unrelated subject matter before I forget. The first time I was going to apply a gel nail polish on myself (and this was barely three years ago), I started doing my research days ahead – I mean, that was my usual way. I had ordered my tools and I had it all pictured in my head: the polish was going to be a sweet nude colour because nudes are one of my favourites. Glue: check; nails: check; gel polish: check; new nail files: check. I wasn't missing anything.

Everything arrived and I started my project on that fateful evening. I had watched the relevant YouTube videos earlier so I knew exactly what to do. I started with the artificial nails and I fixed those successfully. It was my first time doing that myself too so I was very proud of my work. Then I started the painting part, lovely color, I definitely have a good taste. Then I set it down to dry. And this was where it got tricky. Brethren, two hours post painting and my nail polish still hadn't dried. I knew something had to be wrong. My natural instinct would have been to whip out my phone and ask the internet what the problem was, but having wet polish on, I could only do limited things with my hands. Anyway, I managed to grab my mobile phone while unavoidably smearing some of the nail polish – a sacrifice I was willing to pay to end this misery.

Typed my problem in the search box, then it hit me. I had missed something, a major item. Apparently, a gel nail polish will never dry without a UV/LED light. How did I not know this? You mean to say I should have ordered a UV light as well? I was bummed. Long story short, I cleaned the entire polish off my nails - it was already all over the place by now anyway. All of these comic relief to say that there are some mistakes we might be able to avoid if only we'd do our homework diligently in advance or take advantage of experienced counsel. That again brings me to the next point.

10. Have a mentor or someone you look up to

This goes hand in hand with the accountability partner point, only that it's somewhat more specific. A mentorship is a relationship where a more experienced or knowledgeable person helps guide a less experienced or knowledgeable person. There are people who have walked the path you're on. Find them, even on social media and make them your silent mentors (I have at least two people who are silent mentors for me). What can you learn from them? What did they wish they had known when they were at your stage?

In a January 2018 Forbes article, three good reasons to have a mentor are: i) they help you set a measurable goal, ii) they never let you settle and become complacent and iii) they share personal experiences that can inspire and motivate you. Doesn't it just make sense that the road would be easier to travel if we had some kind of tour guide?

There are some people that I try to learn as much as I can from because I see some traces of myself in the paths they've walked or are walking. For a fact, I also make a conscious effort to not copy their lives verbatim because that was never the intention of mentorship. Everyone has their individual life story and no matter how similar our paths might seem, our lives are still wholly different. Our mentors are to never replace God in our lives, or even come close.

This is a common mistake many of us make with mentors and people we look up to. The people we look up to are humans like us and no matter how perfect they seem, we need to cut them some slack - especially since we're experts in cutting ourselves all the slack in the world. I do agree that there might be a minimum expectation from our leaders and mentors but still, we need to come to terms with the fact that the only person who ever walked the face of this earth blameless is Christ. The rest of us, mentors and mentees alike are only striving to be like Him. And isn't it wonderful that we have such an example to look up to? Yet, none of us can fully be like Him until we drop this earthly tent that we have on – something else to look forward to.

We should love and respect our leaders and mentors but we should never idolize them. Like us, they are imperfect people and we will be sinning against God when we respect what humans say over what He says or has said for that matter. Less of 'my mentor/pastor said and so it has to be true', and more of 'God said this and I believe it to be true'. Christ is the only one we are required to model our lives after and He should be our number one role model all day every day.

11. Less pressure; more intention

I once read the story of a lady who passed away due to cancer.

She had her friends and family members present with her in her final days where they delivered eulogies as she listened with tears in her eyes. She wondered if she had fulfilled purpose, she wondered if she made any impact at all in the lives of these people. But as these people described how she had touched their lives in the littlest of ways, she realized she had actually fulfilled purpose and touched lives by just being herself.

It's okay to be who God created us to be. We are complete and capable of living the life He has called each and every one of us to live. Let's strive to be the best possible version of ourselves and not compete with others who have a different assignment on their lives. May we be a generation that is intentional about who we are and who God is calling us to be, not who the world demands us to be. Let's not be carried away by societal pressures of who we ought to be, nobody in this world should define for us who we are. Rather, we ought to surrender to the Lord daily as He writes the story of our lives.

12. Lessen the 'noise' around you

When our son was learning how to walk, we had the time of our lives watching him. He was a little over ten months old when he started making attempts to take those baby steps. On his own, he would stand unconsciously for a while and then my husband would try to cheer him on 'Go Aaron! walk, you can do it!' Very quickly, what was meant as an encouragement would become a distraction to him and we noticed that once he became extra conscious and aware of the excitement and praise around him, he'd just sit back down. He'd been distracted by praise, which normally is a good thing. We had to learn to not distract him with noise if we really wanted him to get comfortable walking on his own.

Sometimes, what ends up becoming noise to us won't even start out as noise. It could be genuine but it may still distract us from a God-given goal. It could be as simple as us sharing a plan the Lord gave us with everyone and then the many compliments we get from people (which again, not a bad thing in itself!) begins to distract us from the main goal (this is where the problem is). Perhaps, we then start to feel like we're doing over and beyond whereas we're just doing what we ought to be doing as children of God. I honestly can't remember how many times I had to get off social media just so I could focus on making progress with this book – it was a big distraction to me and this can be different for everyone. What is it that has the tendency to distract you? It may be coated in gold or dipped in silver but it might still be a distraction to you and your walk with God. Be sensitive.

13. Keep evolving as the Lord leads you

Let's go back to the parable of talents when the folks with five and two talents respectively invested in their talents and their master was proud of them when he arrived since their investments yielded interest. On the other had however was the guy with the one talent who went and hid it. You and I get to determine what we'll do with our God-given talents. I believe that it is our responsibility to use those talents and abilities wisely and efficiently.

As long, of course, as your 'evolution' does not go against God's word (we are not to blend with the world) as long, of course, as your 'evolution' does not go against God's word or change the message you were sent. Honestly, if you have no problem using cars or mobile phones, you probably shouldn't have any problems finding ways to make your work and ministry efficient. We already know that we live in a fast-paced world and there is a continuous invention of tools that can be used to disseminate information better. The devil won't stop taking advantage of these to get his destructive message across to the world, so we - children of God shouldn't hesitate to use available medium and even invent new systems as the Lord leads us, to provide the life-giving message of Christ to the world. Someone on your timeline may just need that word that you have to share.

To be clear once again, God's word is not what is to evolve or change - His word is ever constant and never changing regardless of times and seasons. Evolving for one person might mean learning a new language in order to communicate with a set of people God has sent them to, for another person, it could mean learning a new craft. Whatever it is, I pray that the Lord will guide you to be able to know His pleasing and acceptable will for you in your assignment.

14. Enjoy every season of your life

The books of Ephesians, Philippians, Colossians and Philemon are called the prison epistles because Apostle Paul wrote them while he was in prison. Sometimes, I try to imagine what this experience would have been like for him but again, that's all I can do – imagine. Here I am, typing away in the comfort of my home, at worst sitting on my kitchen floor. Probably treating myself to the luxury of a cup of tea when I need one. And occasionally struggling with my simple problem of finding the strength to finish the work God gave me and concentrating - which usually means that I have to wake up before the world wakes up when I don't want to. But there was Apostle Paul. A prisoner. Doing God's work. In Jail. Perspective. The End.

In the Roman world, imprisonment was hardly a long-term punishment. Most prisoners were either awaiting trial or execution. Paul was looking at the possibility of death while writing those letters. Picture chains, picture harsh living conditions, picture being guarded under the clock by soldiers who had no problem striking you at the slightest provocation. Yet, he still did the work he was called to do in that season: writing letters to the body of Christ. The apostle was eventually executed but those letters he wrote are forever useful to you and me, and will be for many generations to come. What if he'd been so pre-occupied with how terrible his situation was that he couldn't bring himself to write those letters?

He knew he'd likely be killed but how this didn't stop him from encouraging other people (again, while in prison) just baffles me. The one in physical bondage encouraging the ones that have physical freedom - the irony. Yet, to live is Christ, to die is gain! When your focus is on God as opposed to your problems, you may be weighed down but eventually, you'll be able to find joy even in the darkest seasons. The enemy can challenge your faith, take away your money, take away your clothes, take away your family, but he could never take God from you or you from God.

> *"I have told you these things, so that in me you may have peace. In this world you will have trouble. But take heart! I have overcome the world." - John 16:33, NIV*

Nothing can ever separate us from the love of God. You may be in a really rough season right now but look and you'll find God somewhere in it. I may have only spent a little under thirty years on this earth but I've had a few of those moments myself, when I wished it was just over. We'll have tough days (not negotiable) but on those days, we'll need to be able to remind ourselves that God is not only with us, but has a plan for our lives. And His plan is always perfect even if it seems unreasonable or crazy. How are you doing in your current season? Are you able to be thankful for even the littlest things that are working in your life right now? Because I tell you, gratitude in rough seasons although difficult, is the real sacrifice of praise and if we can muster it, it could change our perspective in hard situations.

There's a reason for everything that we go through in life and there's always a lesson to be picked from every season of our lives. Even in God's quiet, He's communicating something to us. Have you noticed that sometimes when you're going through a tough season and you try to pray it away, it just doesn't go away? Those are the seasons designed to help us grow. We cannot pray spiritual growth and training away because they help us mature spiritually. Tough pill to swallow, I know.

"Consider it pure joy, my brothers and sisters, whenever you face trials of many kinds, because you know that the testing of your faith produces perseverance. Let perseverance finish its work so that you may be mature and complete, not lacking anything." - James 1:2-4, NIV

Lol, he said pure joy. How do you find joy when you can barely smile? When you're soaking your pillows wet with tears every night? When you almost feel abandoned by God? But, if we're going to truly find joy in our circumstances, there has to be a shift in our perspective. A shift away from the idea that joy is conditional to the fact that our joy cannot be determined by anything that goes on in this broken world. The fact that our problems and trials do not define who we are. That our consolation is in something greater than everything in this world combined. That we have a hope of glory unlike anything the world has ever seen. It takes a whole level of spiritual maturity (which I'm hoping to attain, myself) to know and believe this but this is the key.

Sometimes, the answered prayer is not in the absence of challenges, it is in the strength that we receive to face and go through those challenges. We'll all have a thorn in our flesh at some point in our lives but God's grace is ever sufficient for us. There might be days when we don't believe that God's grace really is sufficient for us but this doesn't make it any less true. Those tough circumstances are a reminder that we're still physically in this world and we're always going to need God. Don't be discouraged, look on the brighter side of whatever you are going through. Don't try to circumvent the process, it's only for a season, and it just might be your pruning process. The pruning process is painful, I'm not a fan of it myself but there's always a bigger picture.

What counts at the end of the day is what we make out of those seasons. And if there is anything I know, it's that once we survive those tough seasons, we become stronger and better; we are becoming tested and trusted. The idea was never for us to trust in our own capacity. It was and is for us to trust in Him to work in and through us even in the midst of life's problems.

15. Don't be intimidated by the progress of others

You have your own race to run as does everyone else. You are no less than anyone and neither are you better than anyone. This is because there is only one of each of us, and God has called us all to different assignments, in different capacities in this world. While writing this book, I would write about four thousand words on my best writing day and while there were definitely more days when I wrote zero words, I usually felt on top of the world on my good writing days. For a fact, four thousand words is a lot of words to write in one a day but soon enough while I was researching on how to write more effectively, I made an interesting finding. Michael Crichton, the American writer who wrote the *Jurassic Park* novel, was believed to have written up to ten thousand words per day when he was alive.

And then my sweet little pride, the one I felt earlier, shrunk for a little bit. As unimportant as this sounds, I was already becoming intimidated by someone else's journey. Ten thousand words a day is clearly an insane writing output (I mean this entire book is like fifty-five thousand words) but in that moment,

I felt like I was not meeting up to a certain standard. The real question I should have asked myself is what or whose standard was it? Was it God's standard, or was it something I made up in my head because of what somebody else did? I had failed to notice the other amazing writers who wrote an average of one thousand words per day - I'd seen only what I chose to see.

I knew that I wasn't supposed to compare myself with other people so why did I still feel that way? Because of a brief moment of forgetting that I was on a different race. Since then however, I snapped out of that feeling and maintained writing in streaks. There were days when my writing would reflect an explosion of plethoric content and there were days when I just did more of meditating, studying or researching and no writing at all. Regardless of where my writing went each day, I was learning to make the best of each moment and put God and not myself first.

If anything, the progress of other people should encourage us to do better rather than make us feel intimidated or envious. So, when next you find yourself questioning your ability because of somebody else's progress, remind yourself that you're not striving to be like them. Yes, they might have some qualities you could learn from, but ultimately, you are striving to be the best version of yourself that God has called you to be. There's always enough room for all of us to do our part on this earth. There is room for you and you need to take your place if you haven't already done so.

When I started writing this book, I felt like a handful of people had already written or talked about what I wanted to say and I wasn't sure what extra difference this book by poor little me would make. Yet, I felt no other topic impressed on my heart like the one this book is about - for this book, it was going to be either this or nothing. And then I remembered something I saw somewhere: *It may have been said by others but it still hasn't been said by you and that's the difference* and I began to understand things differently. So, stop worrying about the fact that too many people are already doing what God has called you to do. Other people may already be saying the same things but not everyone will hear those people, some will hear only you. There are people; real lives on the other side of your obedience. A lot of people have gone before us and a lot will come after us so why worry too much? Let's just focus on who God has called us to be and be it all.

When we start being genuinely happy about the progress of other people, we will have truly matured. When you hear about the successes of your friends and colleagues, rejoice with them and let it encourage you to do better. If you know within yourself that you've not been living up to God's standard for your life, get up from your slumber. Dust your slippers (you can wear shoes later) and chase after Christ in obedience.

Granted, competition is buried in many aspects of our lives such as work, school or sports, but don't get yourself involved in unnecessary ones. I'd like to chip in that there is something called a healthy competition. It isn't based on fear, envy, diminishing others or a desperate need for validation. It's based on two or more people unlocking their personal potential and motivating one another. Our lives model the lives of the people closest to us so we need to get ourselves buddies who make us want to be better people and vice-versa. Be around people whose lives encourage you to fulfil purpose. Get yourself friendships and relationships that set you on fire for God. That fire can be really contagious!

16. Be consistent

It will be putting it mildly if I said that consistency is hard to achieve. Consistency requires discipline but it eventually breeds expertise since we naturally get better at whatever we do constantly. Consistency is important in goal-setting and strategy because it is a reflection of commitment and discipline. Want to learn how to hear God more? Consistently spend more time with Him. Want to be more physically fit? Find a good work-out/healthy diet routine and be consistent at it. Want to improve a relationship with a loved one? Consistently spend more time with them. Want to excel at your job or career? Do your job well and be consistent at it.

Consistency is a combination of activity and time. What this implies is that there has to first be an activity before we can then start to practise consistency or do it frequently. Your desire for consistency will depend on how much you value those tasks and goals, and it will require your time and commitment.

I was doing some research and I found a few things that are common with consistent people.

1. **They pick their battles**. They don't try to be perfect at everything. They prefer to optimize their attention and energy on select things. Imagine someone trying to be a great singer, engineer, writer, medical doctor, lawyer, accountant, and politician all at the same time. Yes,

some people are very good at multitasking, but most people on the other hand will be more effective when they do only few things at the same time.

2. **They keep their eyes on the prize**. Consistent people like everyone else, get tired. But what keeps them going is their end-goal. Even better when they are children of God and their end-goal is Christ glorified, because their willingness to serve God and the guidance of the Holy Spirit will keep them going. When the going gets tough, these might be the only things that keep us going. Whatever made us start in the first place should be strong enough to keep us going.

3. **When they fall off the wagon, they don't stay down**. Since no one on this earth is perfect, consistent people can fall off the wagon too. What differentiates them however, is their ability to get back up when they fall. They refuse to stay pinned to the ground when life rears its difficult head in their faces - we should learn from them. The Lord never said it was going to be easy; only that it would be worth it in the end.

17. Be prepared for feedback and criticism

Negative feedback is one of the most difficult things to accept. But if we're going to do the work we're sent to do, we're going to have to be tolerant of critiques to some extent. This is something that I personally struggled with in my earlier days of content creation but I've come to the conclusion that it's not avoidable if you want to make any kind of impact. I sometimes read the reviews of a random content and my heart would skip a beat at the brutality of critiques. Don't they teach people how to criticize gracefully anymore? I'd wonder.

Imagine that you have been working on a project for an extended period of time and you finally put it out there only for you to get a handful of negative reviews. And I get it, some or even most negative reviews make a good point but that doesn't change the fact that this can still be a hard pill to swallow for many of us. Negative criticisms could make you to begin to question your calling and decision to put content out there, but I think it helps to realize that it happens to everyone and also that it could help us grow. The fact remains that whatever you put out there (whether it's at your workplace or ministry), whatever message you share is naturally prone to criticism whether you like it or not, because not everyone will agree with your views. And not everyone should.

Because we live in a real world and I'd like for this to be as practical as possible, I think that the following reminders can help us to be mentally prepared for feedback and criticism.

1. **<u>Not everyone will love the work you're doing.</u>** And as long as we're still in the world, not everyone is supposed to. Especially if they are not necessarily part of your target audience. As an example, I personally don't read or watch certain kinds of fiction novels or movies so if I ever stumbled on any of those, the last thing on my mind would be to give a review. The reason is because if the content is by default un-appealing to me, I'd probably have nothing pleasant to say in my review, unless said content is really good. But not everyone thinks this way, others might go ahead and give a

review anyway and it helps to be prepared to encounter those once in a while.

2. **<u>Sometimes your critics are right (ouch!).</u>** I'm not sure which one is more difficult to accept; the fact that you'll get criticism occasionally or the fact that sometimes your critic(s) really might be right. We won't be able to create room for constructive criticism if we've built a wall between ourselves and criticism. It doesn't sound pretty but some criticisms are actually helpful for us because we probably won't always be right. We need to find a way to make sure that we pick any learning points in the criticisms that come our way. Ultimately as Christians, we should maintain an open mind and ask God to direct us to know which criticisms are useful to us and which aren't – which ones align with God's word and are designed to build us up and which do not.

3. **<u>Your mistakes don't define you.</u>** Making a mistake does not mean that God no longer called you. Constructive criticisms should help us go back to God and do better rather than crawl back into our shells. If we realize we've made a mistake, we should own up to it and be genuinely apologetic. If God sent us, He's more than able to pull us through our lowest times. So, back to the issue of differentiating between constructive and non-constructive criticism, I was recently reading the reviews of an amazing book written by the wife of a politician. This book had absolutely nothing to do with politics but to my dismay, some of the critics made it their personal ambition to come on the book review

section and verbally attack the writer and her family – all because of her spouse's political involvement. I was dumbfounded to see this in a 'book review' forum.

I've learnt to say nothing at all if I either have nothing gracious to say or don't think I'm well informed enough to form a public opinion but in these days of social media, everyone seems to have a public opinion and this honestly wears me out to see sometimes. If my criticism will not be constructive, I'll prefer to keep mum until I'm able to put 'constructive' thoughts together. Plus, I have made peace with the fact that I don't have to have an opinion on everything (perhaps someday, we could put this on a sign post).

18. Rest

Anyone who works hard (and smart as we now say) deserves to rest. Because they've earned it and rest is sweet after labour. If we fail to take appropriate rest when we should, our physical bodies will eventually demand that rest from us compulsorily. For someone like me whose mind is almost always spinning, this is a reminder for me to prioritize my rest. I think it's very important to discuss this point because prior to now, I have talked more in this book has been on how we can fulfil God's mandate for our lives and if we're not careful, this can almost sound as though we need to be running helter-skelter all our lives. But that's not the way it should work, that's definitely not the way God intended for us to live. Don't be so obsessed with activities and goals, your overall wellness and wellbeing is paramount to living a fulfilling life.

When we're working on an assignment that we believe so much in, we should definitely give it our all, losing sleep when necessary. But as we do that, we should prioritize our rest and wellness because the human body was not made to work in overdrive perpetually. We need our bodies to function properly in order to continue to fulfil God's mandate here on earth.

So, let the dishes lay in the sink for a little bit, get a spa treatment, eat and sleep well, exercise, let someone you trust hold the baby, delegate some of your tasks. Breathe, just breathe. We need you here, to continue to be that important part of the body of Christ, at least before the Lord finally says come home. But until then, don't be in a hurry to run 'home'. Protect and maintain the temple of the Lord – your body.

V

Getting out of your comfort zone

"I can do all things through Him who strengthens me"

— Philippians 4:13, NKJV

I love my comfort zone - it is the place where there is no stress in this world. In my comfort zone, I can snuggle in and catch up on the missed episodes of my favourite series. There, I can pretend that I have all the time in the world. Have I already said how much I love it there? But as much as I do, I'm afraid I can't afford to dwell there. And neither can you. Because dreams are not achieved in the comfort zone. They might be dreamed up there but never achieved there. The comfort zone is one of the most comfortable places in the world but nothing EVER gets done there.

If it's any consolation, it's actually okay to visit that zone once in a while, at least once during our resting periods. This exception is not only something that should keep us on our toes, but it's also something to look forward to. That we can bask in our comfort zone once in a while without the guilt of lazing around. What we're not allowed to do though is perpetually live there. Like John A. Shedd said: *'A ship in harbor is safe but that is not what ships are built for.'*

I used to hate it when things made me get out of my comfort zone but now it's a challenge I look forward to (at least I try to). If we're going to be intentional about serving God and fulfilling purpose, we're going to have to get used to getting out of our comfort zones. The earlier we realize that we were not called to a life of convenience, the better for us. Now, we're going to look at practical ways to not only help us get out of our comfort zone but also become comfortable with not being in our comfort zone:

1. Overcome fear

At some points in my life, I've felt a sense of inadequacy for certain tasks. I've experienced the daunting fear that creeps into your heart to tell you that you cannot achieve the things that God has in store for you. What about the fear of *will my life not be under more scrutiny once I start to put myself out there?'* (recall we talked about vulnerability and criticism earlier?) Yes, that too was something I needed to be okay with. Fear is the opposite of faith, therefore, it is not of God. Fear will not let us even take so much as the first step because we're so scared of failure and the many other what-ifs running through our minds. Fear will keep us stuck in what appears to be a safe haven but isn't. Fear will prevent us from taking our place and the territories God designed for us. Fear is a feeling that we all may feel from time to time but we cannot let it cripple us. And this is a function of whose voice we choose to listen to.

"Peace is what I leave with you; it is my own peace that I give you. I do not give it as the world does. Do not be worried and upset; do not be afraid" - John 14:27, GNT

You may have heard or seen that *'fear not'* appears in the Bible 365 times. And of course, we've been told that this must be that there's one 'fear not' for each day. Praise God if that was what He had in mind. But ultimately, this frequency of 'fear not' in the Bible just tells me how common fear has been from time immemorial. Whether you currently feel fear or you've ever felt afraid to do something that has been laid upon your heart by God, it might help to know that it is a more common feeling than people like to talk about.

Fear makes us feel like we can do nothing and it will handicap us if we let it. It will make us think that the worst has either happened or is about to happen - make us feel like 'it is finished' because we have nowhere to turn to. I have experienced this feeling. The most annoying thing about fear is that we are almost always afraid of something that hasn't even happened.

I remember one of my worst fear experiences about six years ago. Prior to that, I'd always heard about fear and wondered what people were so scared of (but haha, some lessons are better learnt through experiences). It was not the *'I'm-afraid-of-the-dark'* kind of fear. It was the kind that cloaked your heart with darkness so thick you could almost feel it. It was not a one-day type of fear, it went on for days, then weeks, then months. It was the kind that caused your heart to palpitate. It was triggered by a major threat to my then relationship, now marriage. Worst part, it was health-related and there was nothing either of us could do about it. Talk about a crippling feeling.

It took a while - much longer than I would have imagined, for that fear to wane. But eventually I overcame it. I recited all the scriptures I knew about fear but turns out it's not just about reciting scriptures. It was more of believing what I thought I knew. It was about activating faith – the currency of God's kingdom. That fear did not go away until I completely realised that all my eggs were in God's basket. I was left with no choice than to have faith in Him. I had no plan B and I had to get comfortable with that. These are some things that helped me get through that phase, and points I'd like to remember when next I feel fear creeping into my heart:

i. **<u>Know in whom you believe</u>**. With fear, you have two options: one, succumb to it and let it take over your mind; two, let the word of God dwell in your heart richly and believe His promises to the letter knowing that He is all you have.

"Even when I walk through the darkest valley, I will not be afraid, for you are close beside me. Your rod and your staff protect and comfort me" - *Psalm 23:4, NIV*

Many times, we don't get the true picture of the rod and the staff when we read the above scripture. Shepherds use the rod to protect their volatile flock from predators while they use the staff to guide and correct those that are either stubborn or just oblivious to danger. This is how God is with us; guiding us along the way, in and through the darkest valleys. His word is the rod and the staff - useful for teaching, rebuking, correcting, and training in righteousness. The best part for me in all of this is that through it all, the Lord never leaves or forsakes us; God with us – Emmanuel.

ii. **<u>Remember that God is not out to get you.</u>** Fear is not of God. When you realize that you've begun to entertain this ill feeling, run to Him, not away from Him. He is not about to punish you for your mistakes, Christ already paid for your sins. While you might still experience some natural consequences for your actions in this world (in line with the natural progression of the earth), your comfort can only be found in Him. God is not trying to get even with you, none of us could withstand Him if He was. There is no amount of punishment that He wants to mete out to you that will ever come close to the price that was paid on the cross of Calvary. So, disregard that thought that He's trying to punish you by allowing challenges come your way. Jesus paid the price for everything you have ever done or will ever do wrong. He paid for it on the cross, all of it.

iii. **<u>Realize that you can do all things through Him.</u>** As long as it is God's will for your life, nothing is impossible, absolutely nothing. You can do all things through Christ who strengthens you, and so can I. if He has called you to do something and you feel timid, run to Him and receive the boldness that only His Holy Spirit gives (not the one that comes through alcohol or drugs).

If He has given you an assignment, it's because He knows you can do it. With God, there's nothing like '*I'm not qualified enough*'. It is whom He calls that He qualifies and not the other way round. The way we can fully grasp this fact is by meditating on His word and basking in His presence constantly. When we develop a relationship with God and understand the extent of His eternal grace, we'll eventually understand that there's really no need to be afraid even if fear comes to test us once in a while. God has decorated us with more grace to take on fearful challenges than we know and indeed, His perfect love casts out fear.

iv.   **<u>De-clutter your mind.</u>** It's hard to do anything when our minds are filled with fear and anxiety. Whenever we feel fear, it might be worth it to begin addressing it by taking a deep breath and just getting some fresh air. Not just because it sounds cute but because we need to free up mental space to think clearly and ultimately, to hear God as He speaks. De-cluttering could mean doing away with some old emotions in our minds such as feelings of inability, anger or grudges. It could even mean seeing a therapist where necessary.

Decluttering could also mean organizing relevant

information in our mind in a way that it's not all over the place. Okay, this may sound weird but I sometimes liken my mind to a computer drive where needful information are stored in a safe place while the unhelpful ones go to my mind's recycle bin (no kidding). Because really, think about how you would clean up and organize the information on your computer if you wanted to. You probably want them well laid out and not flying all over the place. All of that to say that the best way to begin to address fear might be by getting a clear head. Fear or no fear, this is a good habit - de-clutter already.

v.　**<u>Face your fears.</u>** Unless you want to run away from your fears, this is the part where you take that big leap of faith. Except if explicitly revealed to us by God, nothing is certain in this life and none of us knows exactly what the future holds. That privilege is reserved for God alone and honestly, I'm glad that it is. If life was a crystal ball where we knew the future with precision, there would be no need for faith. We wouldn't learn to trust God in our situations, we'll instead be dependent on our abilities. The mere fact that I live in this complicated world is a constant reminder of how I need my Lord and Saviour daily.

What's the worst that can happen? This is the question my husband asks whenever we're at a crossroad and we need to make a decision. Even though he makes me roll my eyes whenever he asks this question, it might be a question that we all need to ask at some point in our lives, especially when we're feeling fearful.

If you're anything like me, you will have prayed this prayer: 'Lord, if it's not your will for me, don't let it work out, let it slip through my fingers.' I like this prayer. In fact, it almost sounds like a convenient prayer and here's why: I get a feeling that this prayer sorts of puts on God, our responsibility to make the right decisions. But that's not His job. He won't come down from heaven to make decisions for us, He will only guide us if we let Him. Let's think about this deeply: what if it works out and it's not exactly God's will for us? What if it doesn't slip through your fingers, at least in the meantime yet it's not God's will for us? This prayer almost makes it sound like ease and comfort are the only things in God's will for us but I think we'd be wrong to think that.

Here is what I think is a better option. As children of God, it's our responsibility to be able to discern what His will is. God loves it when we choose Him and that's why He gave us free will - the ability to make choices in life. Ought we not to choose Him over lust, money, pointless fame, material possessions, and even our desires, then? Choosing Him daily above all else, the process of learning and knowing God's will is continuous. As we walk with Him, we get to know Him better and become more discerning; a growth process that never ends. I don't ever want to stop knowing and choosing

Jesus. We learn God's will when we continuously dwell in His presence and keep His word in our hearts.

"Your word, I have hidden in my heart that I might not sin against you" - Psalm 119:11, NKJV

No doubt that we might fall short occasionally (I know I have) but as we mature in the Lord, we begin to better understand His will and ways. Again, what's our favorite check to know if it's His will? "If it goes against His word, it's not His will". He will not lower His standards to accommodate our weaknesses. We're the ones who need to up our game and not stray from Him. I recognize the fact that we live in times of 'my truth', 'your truth' and that's one of the ways to know there's a problem in this world: when the truth becomes relative and we find a way to spiral the word of God to suit our quirks and peculiarities. I wonder what ever happened to 'the truth'? As children of God, we're either going to live by God's standards or by the world's standards. For us, there is no middle ground.

If you feel fear today, speak to God about it. Not because He doesn't already know about it, but because it reaffirms in whom you have placed your trust. One of the most common questions we Christians ask is 'why do I still need to pray if God already knows what I am going through?' But here's what prayer does: It lets you let God. It allows you to officially invite Him into your situation. It expresses your free will of choosing to let

Him into that circumstance, and of course I have one of those analogies again:

Imagine that you were gifted a house by someone. The moment this person gives you this house, the title has passed from that person to you. You've signed the new ownership papers and title documents. Going forward, even the person who gifted you the house legally needs your permission before they can come into that same house that they gave to you. It's the same way with the life and freedom that God has given to us. If God has given you something, it's in your hands now. You get to decide what to do with it because you have a choice. This is why you and I still have to make that decision to invite Him into our lives and situations through prayer. Praying will build us, teach us to be patient, and serve as a fortress for us to face our fears.

2. Start where you are

I know we kind of spent a lot of time talking about fear, so let's move on. The fact that it is called comfort zone does not mean that it is a physical place, although it could be. As such, there is no need to go to a certain place to 'fulfil purpose' except God is sending you to a new location or you're going on a missions' trip. More often than not, the comfort zone is simply a mind-set of utter convenience. For some reason, New Year resolutions hardly work for me so I don't really bother with those. I'm a fan of: if I see a need for improvement somewhere in my life, I start to work on it as soon as I can whether that's at the end, middle or beginning of a year. If I'm making a res-olution, it most likely starts right away - Why would I want to postpone something good till New Year's Day? If God has laid something in your heart, start working on it right away unless you're convinced within your spirit that it's not the right time. Do it where you are, take the baby steps of faith. Let's not be the people who dine with the delayer of time and destiny called procrastination.

If something is impressed upon your heart today, don't push it till next month or when all the kids have left home if you can actually begin working on it sooner than that. How do you know you're still going to be alive by that next month or whenever? None of us knows the exact day and time we'll leave this earth or the exact day and time Christ is coming back to this world. I feel like this mystery of life should push us to do what we need to do while we can. It should remind us to live while we're still alive. To fulfil purpose and destiny.

Want to improve your relationship with God? Start today, start where you are. You don't just wake up one day and bam, you're dripping in spiritual finesse without making an effort. Just like our earthly relationships, building a solid relationship with God takes time and commitment. And we've got to make the investment and sacrifice to get that gold. Has the Lord led you to minister to someone, write a song, or a book? Start today. I get it, you might only have one word right now, start regardless. It doesn't matter what your circumstance is. I've al-ways thought life funny in that while we're wishing our lives were like that of some other people, some other people are wishing they had ours. Why don't we then make the best of our circumstance whatever that may be? Some people wish they were as young and energetic as you are, some wish they could get some time from their single life back, some wish they were married, some wish they had kids, some wish they had better health, some wish they had more money, some wish they weren't as popular. Do you see the spiral nature of life?

There will never ever be a perfect time. Let' stop postponing what we need to do, especially when we have a specific leading to take a step. It may be hard but just start. You might have once felt that nudging to do something, but the moment that nudging went (or so we think), you were back to your ordinary life and you struggled to bring it to back to your memory. And then it became wishful thinking. What undone assignments have you managed to push out of your mind? I pray for the grace to complete unfinished business. Don't waste any more time regretting or wishing you had done things differently. I tell myself this and I believe this to be true for everyone else: *'as long as I am still alive, God still needs me to do something and fulfil a certain purpose.'* As long as you are reading this, no matter how far behind or late you think you are, you still have time. Start NOW (and yes, I'm yelling).

3. Stretch yourself

Try your hands on things you never thought you had the capacity to do. Most of my individual gifts were identified as I did things that were outside of my normal routine. During my undergrad years in Nigeria, I happened to be writing my professional accounting examination at about the same time. Most times, I spent my school breaks staying back at school studying for these exams while almost everyone else went home or travelled. I felt stretched but apparently, I could take on even more. I may have mentioned this earlier that as an undergrad, I was also serving as a leader in my then student fellowship. Not that I was compelled to serve in church (you really can't force anyone to serve), I just felt strongly about serving God in my youth. And I'm thankful to have not only served but also developed a relationship with Him during my university years. My grades in school didn't suffer because I was a Jesus-girl and I was also able to progress well with my professional exams - it was during all of those years that I realized how much capacity I had. This is what stretching does to us.

This is definitely not a call for anyone to pressure themselves into taking up tasks that they know they are unable to handle but there is truth in the fact that we all have more capacity than we think we do. Sadly, we don't give ourselves enough credit for this or even want to find out. Many times, it's not that we can't - it's just that we don't want to. The average human doesn't like to be stretched and any form of inconvenience is not welcome. We want the good life, but not the work it entails. We want the dream marriage, but not the hard work to make the marriage a dream. If you'll never stretch yourself, you'll never know how much capacity you have. Not only the capacity to do, but also the capacity to love – even when we have to extend it to those who are seemingly undeserving of love. This is how we become more like Christ. We can learn to love more people because the Father has given us the capacity to do this. But will we put self aside and put Christ on? Will we stretch ourselves and discover how much capacity we really have?

3. Be disciplined

> *"All things are legitimate [permissible—and we are free to do as we please], but not all things are helpful (expedient, profitable, and wholesome). All things are legitimate, but not all things are constructive [to character] and edifying [to spiritual life]" - 1 Corinthians 10:23, AMPC*

Whether it is the discipline to always chase after God or the discipline to follow those dreams through, discipline will always take us far. If you don't like discipline, you're not ready to get out of your comfort zone. Discipline surfaces in different forms. It might be in choosing not to sleep but instead to start working on that project. It might be in choosing to feed your body with healthy things, it might be in working out even though you hate going to the gym. Indeed, it might be in making conscious efforts to not put yourself in situations that could make you fall into sin. As Christians, that extra layer of discipline will help us be who God has called us to be. It will help us follow His instructions with understanding as opposed to selectively obedience. To be disciplined, we first need to commit to excellence. Committing to excellence answers the question of your motivation. You need to be clear on what you're really chasing after because this is what fuels your discipline or otherwise.

When It's Not a Comfort Zone

So, what if it's not really a comfort zone, just a zone where we feel helpless or hopeless? What if it's a hurting zone or a zone filled with stress and fatigue. I don't know about you but there have been moments in my life where all I wanted to do was just lay in bed. Not because I wanted to lazy around but because I was hurting and could not bring myself to do anything at the time. I'm saying this so that you do not feel pressured into 'doing' when you actually just need to heal first.

On days like these, we're not even in the right frame of mind, talk less of being 'built for more'. We're just trying to get through the day and survive, and honestly in such seasons, that's okay. God absolutely cares about us in those rough seasons, not only when we're doing exploits. There are those gloomy days when we just feel bouts of sadness due to an event or even for no reason at all. I'm sure many of us know this but it's normal to feel sad occasionally. Enough of thinking that we have to be at all-time ecstasy because we are Christians, and that if someone feels sad, they're just not Christian enough. As Christians, there's a balance we need to maintain between feeling all our emotions and not letting our emotions rule our life. David in the bible is one interesting character that allowed himself feel everything he was feeling and he always expressed it to God however he was feeling it. My recommendation is to feel all those emotions but always judge them with the word of God, your emotions can't run your life; feelings are real but they're not always true.

Christ too had a moment like this in the garden of Gethsemane and He didn't ignore that feeling. He let it out; He asked that the cup pass over Him, then He asked that God's will be done. Cry if you have to. Scream if you have to. Don't suppress that feeling. Don't pretend that that sadness that you feel is non-existent. 'Yes' to positive confessions but recognizing the presence of a problem is the first step to solving it. When you recognize that there is a problem and understand what God's word says, you can make His word come alive in that situation and start to confess positively, even if everything seems bleak.

Remind yourself of God's promises to you. Recount those things in your life you're thankful for and thank God for all He has done and will do in and through you. Remember that the joy of the Lord is your strength, ask that His will be done in your life. If you cannot bring yourself to be thankful for anything, take a walk outside and thank Him for nature. Feel the sun on your skin, play with the lilies in the valley, watch the birds of the air in all the splendor the creator clothed them in. Then remind yourself that you are worth more than all of these to God. He will help you get through life. He will see you and me through our tough days.

**If you constantly feel depressed, it's probably time for you to speak with a trusted person and get professional help. That person could be the one God would use to help you through this tough time. Don't think you can handle it on your own; we were not made to do life alone.

VI

Living a Life of Rhythm

"Beloved, I pray that in all respects you may prosper and be in good health, just as your soul prospers."

— 3 John 1:2, NASB

Life is really one thing after the other. There are many facets to our lives and it can be a little difficult to make them all work in harmony simultaneously. How do people make marriages, careers, and ministries all work well at the same time? It's definitely doable and you and I can practise how to do it too. Why do we have God on our side again? I like the way that one of my pastors put it: *'It's not about finding balance in every sphere of our lives, it's about finding a rhythm.'* What a word!

For us to have truly lived fulfilling lives, no part of our lives should have suffered for the other. And God is faithful enough to give us the wisdom to find the best rhythm possible to lead our lives. Is your family or your marriage suffering because you want to be the next big thing in the world? Well guess what? Your family is your first ministry. If you don't show that you care about them, it's hard to believe that you genuinely care about the needs of others and truly want to serve them. Because then, you haven't even been faithful with the little in your household, but there you are trying to take on a whole ministry where other people's lives are involved.

Living a life of rhythm means that we're able to spend our time wisely between all the priorities God has placed in our hands. It means that we are able prioritize appropriately and distribute our time and attention accordingly (truth is we can't give 100% of our time to everything in our lives at the exact same time). It means that we excel at all the things God has called us to do. It means that we give and be our best as much as we can. Indeed, our father wants us to live a good life and prosper in all that we do.

People who live a life of balance (rhythm) have a sense for time and responsibility. They know when to press hard and when to just breathe. They know when to chase after dreams and they know when to pass the baton to the next person to continue. They know when they need to delegate, and they know when to just spend time with their loved ones. They know when to take a pause and they know when to use the re-set button. They know all of these and when they are children of God, they know they don't have to do it all by themselves – they allow the Holy Spirit to teach them.

They understand the place of making time for God; they know that they need to re-fill constantly. They walk with God every step of the way and not just on Sundays. No, they're not perfect and they don't claim to be, they only strive to be better than they were yesterday and it is evident to all those around them. They're also wise enough to know that they can't do it all on their own, and they don't have to. These are the kinds of people that you and I need to become. There's no manual to be able to do this aside from the word of God, and the following are some scriptural tips that I think you and I could use as we continue to pursue the lives that we are being called to live.

1. Prioritise your relationship with the Father

"He must increase, but I must decrease" - John 3:30, ESV

This scripture remains in my personal prayer card and my best guess is that it'll always be. There comes a time in our lives when we honestly have to ask ourselves who or what our number one priority in this life is and for some, today might be that day. If our answer is other than God, we haven't fully come to the right understanding just yet – not even a spouse or family member should be our number one priority. He gave us everything we have including our loved ones so it's okay if they come second to God in our lives.

Earlier, we established that our relationship with God is one that we need to keep feeding throughout the course of our lives. It doesn't have an ending point, only a starting point, and the starting point is the moment we confess Him as our Lord and Saviour and make the decision to truly walk with Him going forward. Truth be told, times will come when we don't just feel up to it, and this happens to most of us. But the key in times like this, is to not dwell in our feelings. Recall that in the previous chapter, we talked about letting ourselves feel all that we're feeling? That's different from sitting in those feelings and letting them take control over us and here's a more detailed answer as to why.

Our relationship with God is not based on 'feelings'. His being God is not dependent on how we feel. He is God because that's just who He is. Don't feel like praying? That's okay, but go ahead and pray anyway. Don't deny that feeling, in fact let Him know you don't feel like it but you're going to do it anyway because you know that His presence and love for you is not bound by your feelings. Don't feel like singing praises or worshipping? Go ahead and do it anyway. Don't feel like studying the word of God? Okay, but go ahead and do it anyway. Had a bad day? There's no better place to "un-bad" your day, so to speak, than in His presence. Our relationship with God will not amount to much until we realize that fellowshipping with Him should not be dictated by our feelings.

It's not about trying to work God into our schedules and personal agendas. It's about submitting our schedules, personal agendas and lives to Him daily. Don't wait till your best and strongest moments before you spend time with God. Do it weak. Do it tired. Do it frail. Don't wait till you have the time, create the time. What if you reduced the time you spent on your phone and on general entertainment and instead devoted more of that time to God?

If we plan to have God in our day, the best way is to start our day with Him. Even if it's just for fifteen minutes every day, setting a regular time where it's just us and Him will keep us in that God-consciousness during the rest of the day. Unfortunately, consistency of this kind is a common struggle for us. I struggle with this sometimes; in between work deadlines, caring for my family, writing a book, recording a song, or just wanting to sleep in a little bit more. Yet, it is something that we must continue to strive for though the flesh be weak.

Isn't it funny how as new believers, we're so passionate about God but then as time goes, we begin to outgrow God like teenagers who become too cool to hang out with dad? Somehow, we've managed to become too busy to spend time with the one who used to be the absolute love of our lives. Just like any relationship, if we don't nurture our relationship with the God, our passion for Him will slowly wane off without us even noticing.

> *"Better is one day in your (God's) courts than a thousand elsewhere. I would rather be a doorkeeper in the house of my God than dwell in the tents of the wicked" - Psalm 84:10, NIV*

Why should we prioritize our relationship with God? The sweet fellowship we enjoy when we spend time with God is second to none. Cultivating a relationship with God will bless us in ways that we never knew possible. In the place of this fellowship, we receive guidance and direction from His Holy Spirit. In this relationship, we find unadulterated joy and peace. The kind that no human relationship could give us. It is the greatest possible kind of joy and peace and the best part is that it's free if only we'll prioritize it.

As a matter of fact, we shouldn't put pressure on any of our human relationships to give us this kind of joy and peace. It's a weight no human could ever carry, and clearly, that includes you and I. We can definitely derive happiness from our loved ones but the earlier we realize that they're not the source of our joy, the better for us and them. Tying our joy to them means we inadvertently give them the power to take our joy away whenever they hurt us (and oh boy, they will). Our best bet is to let our joy come from the one who never makes mistakes, the one who planned our lives from the very beginning. Having a relationship with God is communion with Him and the awareness of His presence in everything around us – in nature, our relationships, and in the tiniest of details.

Or do we want to talk about the things that God can reveal to you in the place of communing with Him? Visions, solutions, ideas, plans. Some time ago, my husband and I were talking about how the distractions of technology today have made us Christians forget that God's supernatural power is still very much alive for us to tap into it. For some reason, this is especially true in the more developed world – perhaps due to the emphasis on self-dependency. Beyond routine dining table blessings, visions, dreams, prophecies are not fables or old wives' tales. They're real revelations that God bestows upon His children when He pleases and as they yield to Him.

Our relationship with God goes a long way to influence our relationships with people. It naturally reflects in our day-to-day activities and relationships, and can be perceived from miles away. I'm yet to meet a true growing child of God who makes it their life's mission to be nasty to people. I'm yet to meet one who doesn't see a problem with lack of integrity, crimes, vices and injustices. God's children are not perfect but because their aim is to be like their heavenly Father, they love what He loves and who He loves (and He loves every individual on earth). They also dislike the things that He dislikes; their minds are gradually being transformed to be like that of their father daily, or at least that is the goal.

Our new life

"Therefore, if anyone is in Christ, he is a new creation. The old has passed away; behold, the new has come"
- 2 Corinthians 5:17, ESV

By virtue of being born into the God's kingdom, we become new people. No, we don't grow taller or fatter and neither do we get a fuller head of hair than we already had. The switch is done in the spiritual realm and nothing really happens to our physical attributes when we become born again. We move on from death into life, from darkness into light. We exchange our sinful nature which has been condemned to death for Zoe – the life of God. Without this life of God, we merely exist with a label that says 'Christian' but are still unable to bear any life-giving fruits.

We all have the sinful nature before we become born again and it's not even because of what we did. Every person born into this world is born a sinner - yes, you were already a sinner before you committed your first sin (thanks, Adam). Sin was passed on to the rest of us because Adam, the first man, sinned. This was a spiritual transaction; therefore, another spiritual transaction has to take place when we give our lives to Christ. Because sin came into the world through one man, it makes sense that God came up with a plan to help us put off that sinful nature through another. Yet, because the arm of flesh always fails, this new man was not just another guy like Adam. He was God in the body of a man.

> *"So you see, just as death came into the world through a man, now the resurrection from the dead has begun through another man"* - 1 Corinthians 15:21, NLT

Until we leave this earth physically, we cannot fully become spiritual beings. This is why we, as believers, still fall into sin sometimes, despite the fact that we've been spiritually changed. Let's dive in a little deeper: the human component is in three parts namely; the spirit, the soul, and the body. Every single person on this earth has all three. The spirit is the part of you that becomes born again at the point of salvation. Your soul is your mind - the place where you put together your thoughts, decisions and choices. Some people have described the mind as the seat of intelligence. Your body is the physical representation of who you are, it is the part of you that can be physically seen and touched. It is the part that physically marks your attendance in this world. As a believer, your spirit is a citizen of heaven while your body is a citizen of the earth. We are left with deciding which one we will gravitate towards: the spirit or the flesh? And we make this decision in our minds.

When you made the decision in your <u>mind</u> to become born again (and hopefully, you have), your <u>spirit</u> crossed to a new state but your <u>body</u> did not change. And this does not negate the fact that divine healings can happen at any point to alter the way a person's body is, for example a lame person could eventually walk. After salvation, the main part of our existence that we need to work on as children of God is our minds because this is where we make the decisions that influence the turnout of our lives on earth.

The mind is so powerful that it determines if a person would go God's way or not. The decisions that we make even after our salvation will be made here. Whether we choose to yield to temptation, inflict pain, or bring smiles to people's faces, all happens in the mind first. Except by conscious effort, our minds remain the same after we become born again since this is where our free will is. Hence the great need for this verse of scripture:

> *"Do not be conformed to this world, but continuously be transformed by the renewing of your minds so that you may be able to determine what God's will is—what is proper, pleasing, and perfect" - Romans 12:2, ISV*

We have a choice to make, of what we will submit our minds to daily. And this is why we're individually responsible for every decision and action that we take (can't blame those on God, sorry). Our minds will either go the way of the spirit or the way of the flesh. And because the mind is so powerful, we need to ensure that we feed it with the right things constantly. We need to see to it that our minds are brought under the authority of the Holy Spirit per time.

As we make up our minds to die to the flesh daily and make it a priority to do our father's will, we will realize that we're becoming more like Him inside out. This is when our minds begin to gravitate more towards God than towards the flesh. Only then, is it safe to say the spirit is winning over the flesh. You may ask: What's the use of trying to regulate our minds when our spirit-man is already born again? Because we're still here on earth (as new beings, we've been changed from being just another individual on the earth to representatives of the Most-High), and our mission on this earth has now transitioned from our personal agenda to God's agenda. When we become saved, we become partners with God and our purpose on earth is now aligned with God's agenda as we yield to Him daily. Due to this, our minds need to be renewed so we can know God's will and make decisions that elucidate who we now represent here on earth. If your mind is still with me at this point (pun intended), you might have the potential to be a scholar. But seriously, I'm hoping that that long-winded explanation made sense to you.

Now, if for whatever reason, anyone is failing in this regard, that is failing post-salvation to understand their purpose to now be in and with God, it's never too late. If we're still alive, it's because our work here on earth isn't done. The worst-case scenario for a believer is that they were saved but somehow, they don't have good works to show for it and didn't bear good fruits. Even then, this doesn't nullify the work of Christ on such person's salvation – they will still make heaven. But since all of our works here on earth will be tested on judgement day, they'll have no good "report card" to show the Master (see verse below). I don't know about you but when my time on earth is done and I have to give account of my life, I want my heavenly Father to be proud of me.

> *"Their work will be shown for what it is, because the Day will bring it to light. It will be revealed with fire, and the fire will test the quality of each person's work. If*

what has been built survives, the builder will receive a reward. If it is burned up, the builder will suffer loss but yet will be saved—even though only as one escaping through the flames." - 1 Corinthians 3:13, NIV

Truth is we're not required to be perfect and can't be as long as we're here- only God is. We make mistakes (I know I do) but the great news as children of God is that our mistakes cannot take away our salvation. In no way did we earn that salvation in the first place and once we're in Christ, we're in Christ. If salvation did not come by our works, we also can't lose it by our works. However, God wants us to lead meaningful lives - surrendered and dedicated to Him, while we're here on earth so we can bring glory to Him and bring more people to Him. And I suspect that the more we're surrendered to Him, the more we can learn to be like Him, and the more we can be worthy representatives of God on earth.

Becoming like Christ doesn't happen by mistake, it has to be done intentionally. It will happen when we learn to yield to His Holy Spirit on a daily basis. Learning to become like Christ does not mean that we will no longer make mistakes – this might still happen because we're still physically living in the flesh. But we live rest assured that even if we do make mistakes, He's always there to guide us back into the light.

Lord, lover, friend, comforter, teacher

Since that fateful day that the veil of the temple was torn in two, all our Saviour wanted was to have a personal relationship with each and every one of us. A relationship that comes at no cost to us. Because of this relationship we now have with Him, He is concerned about every single detail of our lives: our careers, our families, our academics, our feeding, our clothes, everything.

> *"Look at the birds. They don't plant or harvest or store food in barns, for your heavenly Father feeds them. And aren't you far more valuable to him than they are?" - Matthew 6:26, NLT*

Oh wait, you didn't know that God could literally teach you in your day job or school work? I'm not kidding and I speak from a personal experience which I'm about to share. Have you ever been in an examination where you were met with questions that you had no idea where they came from? Not just because they were tough but because you can't recall being taught anything similar and so no amount of studying could have prepared you for what you saw in the exam? I'm talking about the type where you couldn't even guess the answer, you either knew it or you didn't. This happened to me live in my undergrad days.

It was my first year at university and it was an History course. I'd read my class notes from front to back like I'd typically do, and I was feeling very prepared for the examination. Well, at least before the exam started. I received the question paper and that was when it happened. Every student's nightmare. Being faced with questions that you knew you couldn't answer. Obviously, this was not true for every single question on the exam because it would have meant I was either sitting in the wrong exam or I didn't do my part to study as I should have. But the few questions that made me feel this way were the kind I would have left blank because I had no idea what the questions were even asking, I couldn't have guessed the answer. I was even in more shock because I was the type of student you'd consider studious, and preparing for this paper had been no exception.

With History exams, if you don't know the answer to a question, you're probably better off just accepting your fate. The question could look something like: what's the name and nationality of the first person to ever carve out designs from rocks. And the worst part was that for this particular exam, those questions were fill-in-the blank questions and not multiple-choice. So, no way I was going to recite 'ADE BABA CAC' (some of you readers will have to go figure out what this means). I mean, how bad could this examination get! Cheating by way of trying to consult with others during the exam had never been an option for me. Even before I became a believer, I wouldn't do it, how much more now when I was a Christian and my moral compass was in better shape?

But then, something happened. And here's the best part of that convoluted exam experience that day. With my already sunk confidence, I started with the questions I knew and once I was done with those, I sat there for a few minutes before I abandoned the rest, as planned. As I got to that part of the exam paper, I wasn't prepared for what happened next. The answers were LITERALLY dropped in my spirit that day. Not dropped as in 'try either Mufasa or Mansa Musa', dropped as in the exact answers to those questions - names and places I had never heard before in my entire life. I can almost remember this like it happened yesterday and this happened in 2009. If this happened for only one question, I would have brushed it off as a weird coincidence. This went on till I had answered all seven or so questions that I would have hitherto left blank. Call it whatever but this was no mistake or imagination. At the time, I was a new believer still trying to get to know God and I clearly wasn't familiar with strange happenings like this. Yet, I knew something was different. To be honest, I was a little scared at first. When it happened the first time, I thought oh well that's weird. Maybe I had the answer stored in some backend storage of my memory. Then, I scanned around me to be sure the answers were not being whispered by another candidate around me but there was no one even seated that close enough to me.

If not that I was in an exam, I would have asked any of the other candidates in the room if they had heard the voice I heard in my spirit. I knew it was weird to know the answers to questions I'd never read or heard of in my life. Yet, I knew them supernaturally. By God. It was unbelievable, I thought God was too busy for mundane things like a school test. King David wasn't kidding when he said God taught his hands how to war. On getting out of the examination hall, as is common practice, students had gathered to discuss how the examiner was sent from hell to have included questions pertaining to things he didn't teach us. I could relate with the questions being strange but I couldn't explain to anyone how I knew the answers so I mostly kept it to myself. I thought: no one would understand that I'd been taught of the Lord!

"Praise the LORD, who is my rock. He trains my hands for war and gives my fingers skill for battle." - Psalm 144:1, NLT

This was my very first personal encounter with God and I only shared it with very few people prior to now so if you're reading this right now, you might be a special one. With two degrees and three professional certifications, writing exams is something I'm rather accustomed with, and if I say this one time was different, it might be worth it to take my word for it. So, no, I wasn't hallucinating because there might be one or two readers wondering if it was actually an hallucination of some sort.

Has the same exact thing happened again since then? No, but I have definitely seen God's active hand in many other areas of my life, the most recent one being a while back when my family was going through a tough transition period and many things around our next steps were so unclear that it began to bother us. Every decision we needed to make seemed to be hinged on the possibility of something else happening – something we had no control over. The road looked bleak and confusing and so the ambiguity was something we just learnt to live with in that period. We prayed about it but I'm sure many people can relate to the fact that even though you pray about something that's bothering you, it's hard to not worry about it. A few days later, I received a text message from someone in my church back home in Nigeria (for perspective, about 7000 miles away) that the church received an instruction from the Holy Spirit to pray for me and my family. To put this in context, I had not been in contact with this person or really anyone from the church for at least one year before that text came in. Or do I want to start listing all the unbelievable prayers God has answered on my behalf? Or how the inspiration came for the different pieces of this book? Don't let anyone tell you that God doesn't exist.

It's so honoring to know that the God of Heaven and Earth truly cares about us. God works in mysterious ways and we won't all have the same encounters with Him, but in whatever form it comes, it's all still to His glory. There are encounters that you will have that you will never be able to recover from. You wouldn't even want to! Make me recover from anything else, but never the presence of my God. I want to carry it around me everywhere I go.

I can't even remember what the topic was that brought us to this point but let me take a pause here to say: don't get it wrong. I've had a handful of seemingly 'unanswered' prayers too (we call it unanswered, because sometimes God will answer our prayer in a different way than we expected) but even then, I'm so assured that the God of all the earth knows my name and He cares for me. He wants us to relate with Him on a father-child basis. His word and Holy Spirit are there to comfort and guide us. We can tell Him anything, He is there to listen and speak as He will. But we need to be able to recognize His voice for when He speaks or we'll miss out on those important moments. We won't hear God's voice if we're too busy for Him. We won't recognize His voice if our minds are crowded with too many things or worse still, the wrong things since He can't dwell in sin or iniquity.

Irrespective of the fact that the mind is a very important factor in how much of God's presence we get, our minds are not the only thing that can influence our relationship with God. Our physical environments could play a role in determining how much of God we experience. We won't always be able to control what goes on in our physical environments, say, the grocery store. But we can definitely decide if we want to spend every day hanging out with friends in the wrong places. We can decide whether our physical homes will be a dwelling place for the Holy Spirit or not. Let us practise abiding where the Holy Spirit can abide (yes, we have established that He abides in us but I can't help but think that I'm likely to hear God better when I'm physically in a place that isn't repellent to His presence).

Our environment includes the people we chose to spend most of our time with. Obviously, there are certain relationships we don't get to choose (our birth families) but what are we doing with the ones we're allowed to choose? Do we neglect the gathering of believers or are we intentional about spending time with people who want to dwell with the Holy Spirit? God is not bound by environment - He can do what He will anywhere, but because of the free will He gave us, His Spirit will only move to the extent that we're willing to let Him. And to some extent, our minds are influenced by our environments.

Lastly (and I do realize that I've probably written a chapter's worth of words in a sub-section), when we cultivate a relationship with God, we learn to discern. It takes a spiritually conscious person to be able to discern when it is God speaking and when it isn't God even when it looks like 'God's hand'. This is something that I'm continually trying to practise. Imagine an opportunity that looked really amazing and almost every indicator pointed to the fact that it could only be God. Cool stuff, but does it align with the word of God? Is it pure, true and honorable? Do you sense in your spirit that this is the right decision? Beside what things appear to be, as children of God we need to be able to discern whether a course of action is in line with God's will for us or not.

2. Love the people around you

"Love the Lord your God with all your heart and with all your soul and with all your mind and with all your strength. The second is this: 'Love your neighbor as yourself.' There is no commandment greater than these" - Mark 12:30-31, NIV

How can we say we love the Lord when we don't love the people around us? God is not asking you to be besties with every single person you come across but He'd rather you treated them with love and respect. He'd rather you saw them the way He does: as people that He loves and died for. He'd rather you didn't look down on them or spit in their path - irrespective of their beliefs, color or gender. We were not saved for ourselves and God didn't show us His love so we could keep it all to ourselves. We were meant to extend God's hand of love and grace to other people.

The God-kind of love (agape) is not bestowed as a function of people's appearances, career, account balances or religion. And if I'm going to be honest, I'd tell you that this is not a day's job. I'd tell you that it is an everyday job that takes practice and time. Love is something that God wants us believers to practice often. Christ didn't come to die for only you and me, He came to die for every single person in this world. And for me, it helps a lot when I begin to see people around me in that light since it helps me put things in perspective. If they were worth Christ dying for, they're worth loving by me.

So as to leave no room for ambiguity, I'd like to be a little clearer. Loving people with the love of God does not mean loving sin, staying in a toxic relationship, dating out of pity, or keeping bad company. So, yes, you can and should walk away from that abusive relationship but you can still genuinely pray for that person because you have an understanding that God still cares about them. That's love. You can quit your job if you sense God calling you somewhere else but you don't have to bad mouth your previous employer and colleagues on your way out. You can still pray for them, even if they had treated you wrongly. That's love.

There's something that I try to do anytime I feel offended by anyone, asides from talking to them about it when possible - I pray for them. It doesn't really make sense since what my flesh really feels like doing is giving them a piece of my mind and probably never talking to them again (help me, Jesus). But I try to pray for them. In doing this, I realise that I am the one being changed. I am becoming more like Jesus, even in my hurt.

Loving people with the love of God also doesn't mean that you cannot correct or condemn evil. There's probably a bigger problem when you don't. Jesus never overlooked evil, He never swept them under the carpet or pretend they didn't exist. So, what makes us think we should? As Christians, we need to speak up when necessary as we are led to. This includes speaking against injustices, and helping to defend the defenseless and weak. It doesn't mean that you don't love the people who committed those acts, but the wrongful act is what's not to be loved. The God we serve is the God of justice, order, and righteousness.

> *"Instead, speaking the truth in love, we will grow to become in every respect the mature body of Him who is the head, that is, Christ" - Ephesians 4:15, NIV*

We don't need to have an opinion on everything and neither are we called to go around judging people, but we are called to a life of truth in love. How then do we correct people if we are not to judge them? The truth of the matter is that for correction to take place, some element of judgement has to be involved. How would we know that a certain act is wrong if there was no standard of behaviour? Just as every society has laws by which actions are judged and punishments meted out as necessary, so also the Kingdom of God on earth has rules. The word of God is our standard. Now, that's the basis on which we judge if we ever had to.

> *"Do not judge according to appearance, but judge with righteous judgement" - John 7:24, NASB*

Let's not forget that we are also required to be open to correction if we're the problem (and there might be times like this). The fact that we're Christians doesn't mean that we are above reproach. We should learn to admit our mistakes and do better once we know better. The life we're called to live is a life of humility and honesty. It's not a free fall at all. We don't have to be perfect, there will be times when we might get carried away in our own emotions or lash out at the careless driver in front of us. But a few seconds down the line, if we're sensitive, we will find the Holy Spirit convicting us of any behavior that's not like God. If God doesn't stop loving us because of our errors, we shouldn't also stop loving people with God's love because of their imperfections. Let's go back to the word of God and refresh God's love into our lives so we can have it in abundance to share with others even on days we don't feel like it.

How do we practise showing God's love? Let's start with the people closest to us. If we can't show love to these ones, how can we show love to strangers since we're not only supposed to love those who love us right back? We are to love those who don't know or care that we exist just the way Christ, the ultimate example does. Don't wait till you become a boss at work before you make time for your family. For us parents, we already know by now that children grow with the speed of light. So, if we were looking to wait until we become millionaires before we spend time with them or show them that we care, they'd probably be out the door by the then. *'Get as many cuddles and kisses as we can possibly get now'* has always been one of my favorite family mantras and I live it to the letter. Every moment together is a privilege that ought to matter.

Our immediate family members know us better than anyone else. They can tell us hard truths and point out our errors. We need them and they need us (and I get it that some family members can be super dramatic). In most cases, I doubt that they're in our lives because of what they can gain from us. And when we make time to spend time with them, we might be surprised at how much more we learn about ourselves and them.

With loved ones, every minute counts. Don't be so occupied with yourself that you can barely make time out for a phone call. My parents, siblings and I are spread out across three different countries with three different time-zones and it takes an extra effort to keep in touch with everyone. Given this, we try to make it a point of duty to check in with one another every so often through our family group chat. One of the common regrets I hear after people lose a loved one is 'I wish I spent more time with them.' Let's do our best to not repeat that mistake. We never want to look back and feel like we didn't love somebody enough. Now that we still have the ones we have in our lives, let's love on them, let's be there for them. Then we can be truly there for those we barely know.

3. Contribute to society

Since we're not to live for ourselves, we can fulfil some of our mandate by in various ways including donating to the less privileged, visiting and praying for the sick, contributing our time to community activities, or joining a prison ministry. In doing this, we can spread the love of God to people as the light of God shines through us. Let's go out there and be a blessing to our societies too. In the same vein, being good citizens of wherever we live, being obedient to the laws of the land and giving due regard to authorities is part of our reasonable service. Let it not be said that the ones who disregard law and order are the ones who call themselves followers of Christ. When we live in a society, we are largely bound by the rules of that society.

> *"All of you must obey those who rule over you. There are no authorities except the ones God has chosen. Those who now rule have been chosen by God. So, whoever opposes*

*the authorities opposes leaders whom God has appointed.
Those who do that will be judged. If you do what is right,
you won't need to be afraid of your rulers. But watch out
if you do what is wrong! You don't want to be afraid of
those in authority, do you? Then do what is right, and
you will be praised" - Romans 13: 1-3, NIRV*

Once again, this does not mean that you can't speak out against certain laws or practices where necessary - because we live in an imperfect world and our rulers and leaders are humans like us, they can make mistakes too. But when you speak out or take a stand, do so in love and always ensure that your motives are right. This is important because, many of us Christians do not know what roles we should be playing in the society. Personally, I'd rather not be involved in politics and that's okay because as of now, I don't believe that's where God has called me to function but that may not necessarily be the same for you. The world is watching how the children of God will react to certain things. We can't fall short - speak up, pray for your leaders, be a good citizen and above all let your motives align with the word of God. More than anything else, you are first a citizen of the kingdom of heaven. And if peradventure, you ever find yourself in a position to rule or make laws, perform your duties as the Lord leads you. You are not in that position for yourself. You are in that position as a representative of the King of kings.

4. Live a healthy lifestyle

And I'm just going to throw this scripture here for the second time:

*"Beloved, I pray that in all respects you may prosper and be **in good health**, just as your soul prospers"* - 3 John 1:2, NASB

I know that I'd touched on this briefly in a previous section but the truth is that it needs to be repeated. Let's not even pretend that our health and wellbeing doesn't matter because it does. Our health and wellbeing goes a long way to determine how well we are able to function physically. There is supernatural healing in Christ but the supernatural will only overpower the natural when necessary. And who determines whether it is necessary or not? God, not us. He'll heal supernaturally when He wants to and in case you've ever wondered why sometimes we pray for supernatural healing and it happens but other times, it doesn't happen, there's your answer. It's actually not up to you or me.

I had also mentioned in a previous chapter that there's a natural order the world runs by and how this is the way God ordained it to be. For instance, if you are a careless driver, your chances of having a road accident are higher and in the same vein, if you feed healthy and exercise regularly, you may be at less risk for certain illnesses.

God already gave us some measure of control over our health (and I understand that we definitely have exceptional cases) but if this is so, shouldn't we use it wisely to the extent that we can? How have you been using this privilege? How are you keeping your earthly temple? Do you pay attention to what you eat? Do you make healthy choices in life? It can be pretty convenient to ignore our bodies after all, we're now spiritual beings. Granted, we're people of the spirit. However, for as long as we're still living here on this earth, we're still very much in need of those physical bodies.

Our physical bodies are the temple of God (1 Corinthians 6:19) and the vessels with which we will fulfil God's mandate here on earth. Have you been a good custodian of this vessel? Are you doing all you can to ensure that your body is in good shape? Without those bodies God gave us, you can't do anything on this earth, let alone bring people to God. With our bodies, we preach the word of God, minister to people in songs, write a book, talk to people about Jesus, and help those in need. Except you and I can make impact and be invincible at the same time, we better take care of those bodies.

It is not a sin to have medical check-ups or go for therapy – I encourage it. This doesn't show a lack of faith as some might think. I know Christians who have not stepped foot in a clinic for years because of their level of spiritual walk, but this won't be the same for every Christian. Thankfully, this isn't a determinant of who makes heaven or not. Once we accept Christ as our Lord and Saviour, we become citizens of heaven and from that moment onward, it's no longer determined by anything that we do or don't do. While we're on earth though, we're responsible for how we use our physical bodies. It is the earthly repository of who we are and it obviously carries us around. We need to be good custodians of these vessels as service to God, and in order to stay alive for those who need and love us because the greatest gift we can give our loved ones and this world is our presence.

5. Give your best at your place of work

For even when we were with you, we gave you this rule: "The one who is unwilling to work shall not eat." - 2 Thessalonians 3:10, NIV

By now, you probably already know that the words 'Christian' and 'lazy' don't go well together. What's your attitude at work, in your business, or in your school? Are you working/schooling/volunteering with a sense of purpose? You have a choice to decide what job you'll take or what business you'll run and in doing this, it's important for you to be aware of what your motivation. What are your reasons? What really drives you? What motivates you to get up and show up each day? And I get it, we all want to be highly paid for whatever we bring to the table (I know I do) but are we doing everything we do as service to the Lord or are we doing it grudgingly? Are we being faithful with little?

The reason why it's important to know what your motivation to take that job or do that business is because this is what will help you to stay the course diligently while at it. Are you functioning at your best in your chosen work? If not, what are the things you need to put in place to ensure that you are? Are you stressed out? Are you distracted? Or do you just hate your job? I believe that even if you're going to leave your job soon, it's honorable to do the best you can in that present season – in that job, while you still hold it.

How diligent are you at work, business, or school? Christianity aside, anyone paying your wages or salary or for whatever service expects you to do your job. And this means that if you're being paid to do something, the least you can do is to deliver (that is, if you can't go over and beyond expectations which is the ideal thing). And if for any reason, you're unable to perform your job or task at a particular time, communicate properly. If you know it's something that you definitely will be unable to do, you should either do what it takes to get the required knowledge for that job or honorably resign from that job.

According to the *Oxford Universal Dictionary*, diligence is 'careful attention, industry, assiduity, unremitting application, and persistent endeavour'. Diligence is giving your best to whatever you do to ensure the task is done. It is not only working hard but also working smart. At the end of the day, if diligence has really become our lifestyle, we can't really separate being diligent Christians from being diligent in other aspects of our lives. Like someone said: a good Christian is a good "anything", and I'll let you fill in the blank. Being sub-par is just not in God's DNA which we also now carry.

To be effectively diligent, we need to keep learning: this is how we develop ourselves and get better at what we already know how to do. Learning is a continuous activity – I like to refer to myself as a learner for life. We can learn when we ask questions, do some research on our own, take a new course, certification, or go to school. Learn more about your industry, the environment your company operates in, the needs of your customers, whatever is value-adding. Aspire to be excellent in all aspects because that's what your heavenly father would have you do.

It's also important for us to maintain a good relationship with our colleagues and clients regardless of our differences. We can't be acting haughty or rude and expect a good relationship with the people we work with. Be a problem solver, a reliable employee or employer as the case may be, be honest in your dealings, and be ready to provide help and insight when needed. Prioritize your tasks and don't take on way more tasks than you can handle because you want to look good, learn to politely say no and communicate effectively. Watch your attitude, be personable, don't be a people-pleaser (it's exhausting), be vocal but don't be the office gossip, set realistic targets, pay attention to details, go the extra mile whenever you can, ask questions when in doubt. Take time out to catch your breath and rest, don't carry over your vacation days except when completely necessary. Don't get involved in unnecessary office competition or strife. Never forget that you are not in that role to put up a show for anyone, you are a child of God and that's more than enough reason to live a life of excellence. Thanks for coming to my work-place ethics ted talk.

Of a truth, we will meet difficult people along our path or wherever else. Honestly, some people will just hate your guts. Although I'm something of an introvert, it's usually not that difficult for me to make friends with people - but even then, I've met people who just didn't like me. And I know it doesn't feel good when we have this kind of situation to contend with, but it's probably inevitable - Jesus wasn't liked by all. So, let's not allow the negative things that people do to us change who we are and who God is continually calling us to be. Let's not give our power away by being reactionary to the negative things we come across daily. Instead, let's keep our emotions in check and prepare our minds for the unexpected because they will happen. Do your best to be at peace with all people but also be at peace with God and yourself. Then, breathe and rest in the assurance that God's got you for life.

VII

Your Finances and You

This was probably one of the most difficult chapters for me to write because I had to break away from many of my preconceived notions. But I'm very thankful for the things I learnt while putting this chapter together. So now, we talk money: how we can get it the right way, how we can put it to use the right way, and how to not make it a god in our lives. As a finance manager, I probably know one or two things about money but now, we'll place the word of God side by side as we take this journey into our finances. Earlier, we talked about our motives for wanting to fulfil purpose and how that if we're going to do it God's way, our primary motive in life cannot be money – since it'll have to be something deeper than that, something bigger than us. If we're primarily led by our bellies, we're not ready to live the life that God has called us to. That being said, how do we ensure that we're chasing the right things, while making money since it's a necessity?

I think that a good place to start is in realizing that our provision is found in God. He will fund whatever He started to completion, this is His principle and He never reneges on it. God has a way of just providing for His own as long as you're diligent in the path He has set you to be on. I find this very comforting and I think it should not only put our minds at rest, but also encourage us to go deeper in our walk with Him. Whether it is in giving us ideas that will turn into a source of income or in raising people to bless us when we least expect, we can be sure He'll meet us there. I continue to work hard to earn my living but my general principle is that: 'If the Lord has not given me, it means I don't need it'. Not only in my finances but for every single one of my prayer requests. And I am yet to meet one person who truly walked with God and regretted it.

I remember a great book I once read and highly recommend: *Rees Howells Intercessor* by Norman Grubb. This book was a biography of Rees Howells, the British missionary who founded the Bible College of Wales. There are a ton of experiences in that book of how God supernaturally provided for him, even on days when he had no idea where the money for a project would come from. That book is ultimately about a life of faith. This man founded the Bible College and bought several other lands for the Lord's work with next to nothing in the bank. And the best part? He never had to beg anyone for money. We serve the God who can wake someone miles away from their sleep just to make sure that another of His children is not lacking resources. He is God and His word never returns to Him empty. If He says He will do a thing, we better believe He will. He will always fund His work; all we need to do is partner with Him.

Because it is such a necessity, money is actually an important subject and it's impractical for us to act like it doesn't matter just because we're Christians. I don't know of anyone who never used money, alive or dead. We need it to feed, put a roof over our heads, clothe ourselves and our dependents, we need it for ministry. And because of the versatility of what money can do, it can easily become a master in our lives if we aren't watchful. Money when handled well can be such a blessing but on the other hand, can be a detriment to us and others, when mishandled. We've seen money or better put, the love of it sow discord between friends or family members. When it comes to money-related issues, it's easy to lose our discipline and self-control (understood in Nigerian vocabulary as *home training*).

The obsession of money can lead to envy and bitterness. It's sad but many people would do anything – cheat, lie, steal, even kill, just to get money. Poverty is not an excuse for such wickedness. There is no excuse for allowing our lives to be driven by money, especially as a child of God.

> *"For the love of money is the root of all kinds of evil. And some people, craving money, have wandered from the true faith and pierced themselves with many sorrows"* - 1 Timothy 6:10, NLT

The above verse says that the love of money is the root of evil and not money in itself. And I think the reason is because the same money can be gotten and used in honorable ways. Money is one of the things God can give to us but it's definitely not the only thing. So, if God is the giver of money, should we not be chasing after the giver rather than the gift?

Know that God can and will provide for you in ways

beyond your imagination, but this won't happen if money is the only reason you're coming to Him. He's not a magician or money doubler. He is God and more than anything, He wants your heart. He wants you to come to Him because money or not, He loves you. Similar to our human relationships, if we're only in a relationship with someone because they're rich and can make us wealthy, we don't truly love them. Relationships become unhealthy when all we're thinking about is the material things we can get from the other person.

At the same time, God did not intend for us to starve because we're serving Him either. Far from it - He loves us and has wonderful intentions towards us. He blesses the works of His children's hands and wants us to have all that we need. Since He promised to supply all our needs according to His riches in glory, why don't we walk with Him if we have such beautiful assurance?

"For I know the plans I have for you,' declares the Lord, "plans to prosper you and not to harm you, plans to give you hope and a future" - Jeremiah 29:11, NIV

When God gives us an assignment and we choose to do it, all heavenly and earthly resources that we need will be mobilized for us to accomplish it, no matter how tough it might seem. It'll take a big exercise of our faith but it will happen - we just have to give our unrelenting Yes.

God's desire to provide what we need

"For Scripture says: Do not muzzle an ox while it is treading out the grain, and the worker deserves his wages" - 1 Timothy 5:18, NIV

This verse of scripture tells us how important it is that anyone who is working receive their due compensation. This definitely includes you and me (and your spiritual leaders because I hear some of us have issues with spiritual leaders getting paid). We are to not further strain people who are already putting in effort and time to serve by withholding due compensation. Whomever toils deserves to eat, and very well too.

Hard work requires sacrifice including time, effort and even money, and it's only proper that everyone who works to earn an honest living be compensated. So, whether you're a career person, an entrepreneur, or whether you are in full time ministry, God understands that you have bills to be paid and dependents to be cared for.

To reiterate a point I made earlier, God wants us to have all that we need and this is not the same as having all that we want. This means that we might want something we don't necessarily need and are able to do without it. If we're comfortable enough to be able to fend for ourselves and our dependents, we should be grateful. Maybe it's time for us to stop whining about all the things we don't have and quit comparing ourselves to others. It doesn't cost God anything to make us stinking rich but this doesn't mean that He would make us all rich. Truth is we all have different capacities to handle wealth and the Lord knows this – I just think about how easy it is for us to feel like we run the world when we have lots of money at our disposal, even for a brief period of time. It's human nature to feel like we don't need God, we can provide everything we want for ourselves anyway. But what great disservice we'll be doing to ourselves if this was the way we thought.

Obviously, not every rich person is a believer, but believers can definitely be rich too. Contrary to the popular belief that the richest people in the world are not Christians, you might be surprised to learn that a greater percentage of the world's millionaires are Christians. In 2015, the CNBC published an article titled 'the religion of millionaires' and the article cited facts from a study carried out by a research firm (New World Wealth). The study found that of the 13.1 million millionaires in the world at the time, 7.4 million (or 56.2%) identified themselves as Christians. I honestly didn't know that. While we will not all be millionaires or billionaires, it is the will of God that we do not beg to survive.

"Every good and perfect gift is from above, coming down from the Father of the heavenly lights, who does not change like shifting shadows" - James 1:17, NIV

We must not forget that beyond making money, God wants us to fulfil purpose and bring glory to Him because He's our maker. Anybody in this world, anyone at all, can be rich but not everyone will fulfil purpose. God is seeking true worshippers - who will worship Him in truth and in spirit. Not the ones who come to Him for material possessions only. He wants the ones who come because they recognize that He is the giver of all life and in Him alone is salvation found.

I've experienced a number of financially tough times in the past but when all was said and done, God always came through for me. My confidence is in God and not in my abilities. I'll never stop trusting Him, because I know He has my best interest at heart even when it doesn't appear so. Where is your trust? Is it in your skills, job, another human being, or is it in God? Do you live your life believing that despite what happens to the economy or your investments, God has your back?

Godly principles for our finances

1. Recognise that everything that you have comes from God.

> *"For who makes you different from anyone else?' What do you have that you did not receive? And if you did receive it, why do you boast as though you did not?"*
> *- 1 Corinthians 4:7, NIV*

Every good and perfect gift comes from God and for us, it is God who prospers our handiwork and lets it materialize into money. But like we discussed earlier, you can actually have money without believing in God – you just have to work hard and add a dash of luck. It's a natural earth principle that will work for anyone but for the Christian, you don't need a dash of luck, what you get is God's grace and favor to bless the work of your hands.

If we say Jesus is the Lord of our lives, then we have to surrender everything in our lives, our money inclusive. He is the one who brings the super to our natural.

"God is able to bless you abundantly, so that in all things and at all times, having all that you need, you will abound in every good work" - 2 Corinthians 9:8, NIV

2. Be a giver

"Give, and it shall be given to you; good measure, pressed down, and shaken together, and running over, shall men give into your bosom. For with the same measure that you mete with it shall be measured to you again" - Luke 6:38, KJV

Charles Ellicott, a late theologian and academic explained this scripture in his Bible commentary. Here's how he put it (my additions are asterisked and italicized):

- **Good measure, pressed down** – 'The imagery points to a measure of grain, so pressed and shaken that it could hold no more'. **That's how much will be added back to the giver.*
- **Into your bosom** – 'The large fold of an Eastern dress over the chest, often used as a pocket'. **The kinds of clothing worn in those days.*
- **With the same measure that ye mete** - 'Just like in Mark 4:24, this furnishes a good illustration of what has just been said as to our Lord's method of presenting the same truth under different aspects. In the Sermon on the Mount it appears as the law of retribution, which brings pardon to those who pardon, judgment without mercy to those who show no mercy. Here the law works in another region. With the measure with

which we mete our knowledge, God will in His bounty, bestow more knowledge upon us....'. *Essentially, we receive based on how we give.*

Rees Howells (recall from earlier) was reported to have made a certain comment when he was alive with respect to giving and receiving from God in faith: *'There is a golden rule in the life of faith, that the Christian can never prevail upon God to move others to give larger sums of money towards God's work than he himself has either given or proved that he is willing to give if it were in his power to do so.'* I find those words very, very profound.

My mum, one of the most generous people I know, once told me that if a person was tight-fisted, not only would money not leave their hands; money would also never come into their hands. Although a metaphor, this too is true. If you've ever doubted the importance of giving, I'd like to encourage you today. It pays to be a giver, not because your money might be doubled but because it's an actual privilege to be able to give to others. Do not give to receive, give because you love and because you recognize that God is the owner of everything that you have anyway. God loves a cheerful giver and if we will give grudgingly, we're better off not giving at all.

And can I just mention that reaping doesn't always come monetarily. The fact that we gave money doesn't mean that God will always bless us back with money, there are so many other ways that God can bless us. Many of us have become so comfortable in the habit of not giving because we feel we don't owe anyone what we toiled for. And while that is true to some extent, as children of God, we owe God everything and as such,

God doesn't give us money for ourselves alone. We ought to always extend His hand of grace to others in whatever capacity we are able to. There's actually another interesting category of people - those who don't give but also would rather only collect from others perhaps even taking it a step further to demand that others give to them as though they were owed money. When we think that people are obliged to keep giving to us (just because they have more money than us), what we have is called entitlement mentality and this attitude is not from God.

For my peace and sanity, I like to remind myself that nobody owes me anything (except they actually do in reality) so that if and whenever anyone ever gives to me, I am able to appreciate it better. And for me, this not only applies to money. I know some of us grew up hearing: one good turn deserves another. Agreed, but I'd like to encourage us not to expect a return of favour when we give or do things for people. Instead, let us continue to do good because that is who we are and it pleases our Master. It is definitely more blessed to give than to receive.

Giving is a position of the heart, there's always someone we can give to regardless of our own situation – even if it's not in the form of money. We can always give out of the little that we have. That being said, we can't give what we don't have or give out what belongs to someone else without their permission. If we rob someone to give to another, it's not only fruitless work, but we're also in sin and this is not what Christianity teaches.

We shouldn't wait to give only when we're buoyant with wealth. If we choose to wait until we become millionaires before we give, we're missing the point. In order to make giving a part of us, we have to be intentional and as always, we can practise the act of giving with the people around us. If we see a need in someone's life that we can fill, let us try to be a blessing to that person as much as we can. Not because we owe them anything but because that's what God would have us do. God will probably never directly credit people's bank accounts with money. But you and I can and should, since we're His hands and feet here on earth. You and I are the proof of someone's answered prayers.

****

Where your treasure lies, there your heart lies

Before we conclude this section on giving, I thought it might be helpful to talk a little about our treasures and priorities. When did you last check your bank statement? Where does all or most of your money go? Aside from basic living expenses, where has the bulk of your money gone to in the past month? The reason it's important to ask ourselves these questions is because we are what we spend on. We can't say we love God when we're not sharing our time and resources with His work and the lives of people.

How well do we give towards God's work on earth and to people in need? God has no need for our money; He doesn't need our food, clothes or money. But our serving is in our giving and giving is one of the ways that we fill a need in the lives of the people around us and towards God's work on earth. God will always take care of His business on earth but the question is whether we're willing to be the vessels He'll use or not.

"I was naked and you clothed me, I was sick and you visited me, I was in prison and you came to me.' Then the righteous will answer him, saying, 'Lord, when did we see you hungry and feed you, or thirsty and give you drink? And when did we see you a stranger and welcome you, or naked and clothe you? And when did we see you sick or in prison and visit you?' And the King will answer them, 'Truly, I say to you, as you did it to one of the least of these my brothers, you did it to me." - Matthew 25: 36-40, ESV

Giving is a form of worship and it lets us express our gratitude for the fact that everything we have in earthly possessions has been given to us by the Lord. It is one of the ways that we return the glory to Him. We could never repay Him for His love and His gift of salvation. Instead, the way that we show our gratitude is through our worship and by replicating His love to other people on earth. I have learnt that the act of giving itself opens more doors for us than we could ever open for ourselves. This is not why we give but this can be encouraging for someone out there to trust the process.

3. Save and invest

"The wise store up choice food and olive oil, but fools gulp theirs down" - Proverbs 21:20, NIV

I had my bachelor's degree in accounting, so it's probably not strange that I certainly think saving and investing are very good principles. To top it all, the word of God encourages this (a win for my professors). Most of us probably know this already but not all the money that we earn should be spent on daily expenses. There should be a percentage that goes toward different sections. What portion of your monthly income do you let yourself consume? What portion do you re-invest? What portion do you save? What's your consumption-savings-investment ratio?

> *"Send your grain across the seas, and in time, profits will flow back to you" - Ecclesiastes 11:1, NLT*

For the benefit of readers who have no idea what I'm talking about, the major difference between savings and investments is that savings are funds typically set aside for emergencies while investments are funds set aside to re-create wealth or acquire capital assets. You might want to have a savings fund of about six months' worth of your expenses so you have something to fall back on in case of unforeseen circumstances. Savings therefore are typically more accessible to withdraw in contrast to investments. Money invested will likely carry more risk, but also typically yield more interest than money kept in a savings account. The most common kinds of investments are real estate, stocks, bonds, mutual funds or any combination of those, and people put their money in these assets with the expectation that their investment will yield returns on their invested capital. In much simpler terms, you can almost think of investing as you borrowing an entity some money and then they pay you some interest on that from time to time. Well, except that sometimes, you could receive negative interests too.

Some refer to investments as the money that your money makes for you, or the money you make while you sleep. It's not completely a walk in the park though. The major downside to investments is the possible fluctuations in the prices of those assets you've invested in and in the downside scenario, this could lead to a loss on said investment. One way to mitigate this is by diversifying your investment portfolio, and guess what? This advice has long been in the Bible before we came up with business school or investment classes. Just listen to what the wealthy King Solomon said:

"But divide your investments among many places, for you do not know what risks might lie ahead" - *Ecclesiastes 11:2, NLT*

Investments come with different levels of risks and while we all have different risk appetites - or what is called risk aversion coefficient, it doesn't change the fact that investments can be quite rewarding. It's worthy to note that you do not need to invest in something just because that's what everybody else is doing. It takes careful consideration and some people would even employ the services of a broker. I'm sorry if I just bored you with a lot of financial lingo – I'm done now. Kind of.

God is interested in the tiniest details of our lives and this includes the kinds of investments and savings we make. It is important to note that just because we are trying to save up does not mean that we have to live in penury. Yes, we can sacrifice a couple of things pending when we meet a specified savings target but this should be after the basic necessities of life have been met. Afterall, the future really does belong to God.

4. Take on less debt

*"Just as the rich rules the poor, so the borrower is servant
to the lender" - Proverbs 22:7, NLT*

For those of us who live in credit societies that are kind enough to let us buy now and pay later by encouraging usage of credit cards, we all know how easy it is to fall into a roller coaster of debt. Of course, debt is almost unavoidable for major expenses like buying a house, academic tuition, or for starting a new business. Yet, the concern is that an increasing number of studies show that the number of people who are eventually unable to pay off general (consumer) debts is on a rise thereby leading to many people having to file for bankruptcy from general debts.

Living in a credit society definitely has its advantages, and sometimes we won't even have a choice but, we won't be doing ourselves a favour when we fail to exercise self-control in our use of credit facilities. Use credit facilities if you have to but watch your credit utilization (the percentage of your credit limit that you're using which is usually recommended to be no more than 30%). Do you find yourself buying things you don't really need – just because you have a credit card to throw those expenses on? We are called to resist this kind of temptation too. Less of impulse buying (and anger-buying, where applicable) and more of intentional spending.

A good check is to always ask yourself if you're able to finance your current lifestyle with your own actual money. If you answer in the negative, you might want to pay attention to how you spend on the things that are not immediate needs but wants that only cause buyer's remorse down the line. Living within one's means is a skill. If we cannot afford it and we don't urgently need it, we probably shouldn't rush into purchasing it.

5. Be content

"But godliness with contentment is great gain" - 1 Timothy 6:6, NIV

This is one of my favorite scriptures. Contentment does not mean that we are not forward-looking or don't have a desire for things to get better. It means that we're able to find joy in our present circumstance. Contentment means making the most out of a current situation rather than grumbling about all the things we don't have. It means that despite the fact that we may not have as much as we'd like in our bank account and investments, we're not wearing a gloomy outlook. Instead, we remain excited for what God has in store for us knowing that if He hasn't given us yet, it's because we don't need it yet.

Rejoicing in every circumstance is absolutely worth practising. Financial wealth or not, we are called to live a life of faith and dependence on God. Are we content in knowing that we've been blessed with every spiritual blessing in heavenly places? Are we faithful with little or are we busy grumbling that what we have is too little for us to do anything with? Are we silently upset with God for not giving us as much money as the people around us have?

Contentment is the act of being fulfilled while maximizing our present circumstances. It helps us distance ourselves from contempt, bitterness, and envy. The thing is that money cannot make us truly fulfilled in life anyway, and it won't solve all our problems because it was never meant to. This is why some people are financially rich, but they still live empty lives. Water the soil where your feet are currently planted because the grass is not always greener on the other side. It is so soothing to know that whoever has God has everything - a reminder that all of this earth will pass away and everything in it; riches, property, every single thing. Our posture should always be one of thankfulness and contentment, trusting that God has our best interest at heart as we store up our treasures where it cannot rot.

VIII

Laying Aside Every Weight

"Therefore, since we are surrounded by such a huge crowd of witnesses to the life of faith, let us strip off every weight that slows us down, especially the sin that so easily trips us up. And let us run with endurance the race God has set before us."

— Hebrews 12:1, NLT

As you probably know, life is not a bed of roses - or maybe it is, since roses have thorns. You will always have many reasons and excuses to not live that life that God has called us to live. Yet, you cannot afford to succumb to them. Of a truth, some things will come easily to us in life but for others, we'll have to make the extra effort to get it – most good things require the sacrifice of our effort and commitment. If we're not going to achieve something we felt led to, let it not be because we didn't try hard enough.

It's such an irony that as I wrote this exact chapter in 2018, I was diagnosed with a breastfeeding condition called vasospasm

- I was still nursing my then baby. It was as though the Lord was really trying to make me understand what it meant to actually lay aside every weight. This sharp stinging pain would start at exactly thirty minutes after I finished nursing him. Then for the next two to three hours, I would continue to writhe in pain and agony. I had never seen anything like it; it happened every day for almost two months. If I nursed my son three times in a day, that meant six hours of this pain, every single day. I began to feel like pregnancy and child labor were nothing compared to this experience.

Unfortunately, the symptoms were similar to that of another condition; breast thrush, so I was misdiagnosed for having that instead. So, it turned out that I was being treated for something that I did not have (sigh).

Because of how bad it was, my husband advised me to stop breastfeeding at this point but I hadn't planned to stop breastfeeding my son at nine months old (and this decision will be different for every mom). Little did I know that the solution to this condition was not far-fetched at all. Apparently, it could have been solved by just adjusting the way my baby latched onto me when he fed, something that a lactation consultant could have easily helped with.

By the time I realized what the solution was, my baby had given up the whole breastfeeding thing altogether. The poor boy woke up one day and decided he was done with the drama altogether. I was devastated on the one hand because I wasn't mentally ready to stop breastfeeding him. On the other hand, I was exhausted from the pain I was going through. In summary, this was how the painful two-month episode ended after which I finally resorted to pumping milk before we eventually stopped the nursing process altogether.

I'm telling this story for perspective: I developed this condition from nowhere, at a time when I was writing a book that I thought God had led me to write, for crying out loud. I didn't think I deserved to go through that; was writing a book while nursing a baby not already hard enough? But what that season made me realize is: the fact that you're walking in your calling or fulfilling purpose certainly doesn't meant your life will be perfect. If I'd stopped writing this book at that time, I felt like I would have been justified. But one of my mantras in life is that as long as it is still within my power, I'll put in the required effort to accomplish the assignments in front of me - no matter how hard, except I can absolutely no longer do so.

That breastfeeding condition eventually went away after I was forced to abruptly stop nursing my son, but about a month after, my entire family came down with the flu; and this new thorn in my flesh lasted a few weeks. All of these, while we were planning to move to another country; I just couldn't make all these roller coaster events up. The way many different things that could have made me quit writing this book started to spring up one after the other had me like *'devil, get behind me'*. Interestingly though, all of these issues of life will have probably still come up even if I wasn't writing a book; I mean, it's just normal life stuff. We were never promised that the road will be easy, only that it'd be worth it.

I'm learning to live each day like there is no promise of tomorrow because that's just the fact. None of us has the promise of seeing another day, we're just living on borrowed time. People die at any age, time or place and we don't get to negotiate this. When it's our time as believers, it is time. This is why we must make every minute of life count. What's stopping you from fulfilling purpose and from doing the things you know you're supposed to be doing?

Let's take a look at some of these 'weights' in detail:

1. Lack of time
2. Uncertainty
3. Lack of motivating company
4. Lack of funds
5. Random distractions
6. Ill health

1. Lack of time

They say you make time for what you love. I think this is true (refer to that scripture that says where your heart is, there your treasure lies). Like me, you probably need thirty hours in a day. But I feel like even if we had thirty hours in a day, there'll still be many things competing for our attention as there are now. The real question hence is: what are the things we're willing to make time for?

In his book *Eat that Frog*, Brian Tracy writes that the purpose of time-management skills is to enable us spend more time doing the things that give us the greatest amount of joy in life and with the people we care about. He says that if you eat that frog (metaphor for the toughest or most unpleasurable task) early in the morning, nothing worse will happen to you the rest of the day. I probably won't have thought of a task as a frog but I think Brian makes a good point. Do what you need to do as early as possible. There is no shortcut to these things, you have to make out the time and put in the work. We don't wake up one day and like magic, realize we have lived a fulfilling life without us even trying. Time is the minimum requirement to achieve every good thing in life.

I know you have to work three jobs and do a ton of house cleaning but don't forget to take a step back in the midst of all these and ask yourself whether you're truly fulfilling purpose on those jobs or just running a race you didn't ask for. We've talked about the fact that although God wants us to excel in our chosen careers, fulfilling purpose is less about the money we make, and more about the positive impact we make in people's lives. How do you make godly impact if you can never find the time? How intentional are you about the use of your time? Why will you be spending hours scrolling through Instagram when you have a masterclass to start, a ministry to start, a book to read or write, a degree to get, actual relationships to build, lives to impact? It's not wrong in itself to surf social media but many times, we lose sense of time while doing this - and let's not even talk about the social media addiction of this generation, and that's what's wrong. We have no business loafing around if our God-given assignments are left undone.

"Look carefully then how you walk, not as unwise but as wise, making the best use of the time, because the days are evil" - Ephesians 5:15-16, ESV

I don't know about you but I don't want to look back and wish I'd made better use of my time than I did. With every opportunity you get, take a step closer towards that dream that God gave you. Hold on firmly to that dream and start gradually. As long as you're closer today than you were yesterday, you're making progress. The ability to allocate our time appropriately to different parts of our lives is definitely a important skill to learn in our generation.

I officially started writing this book in August 2018 but by September, I had to take two months away from writing so that I could prepare for an examination I would sit for in November. After my exam, I went back to writing my book although it clearly didn't get published till another three years later because life continued to happen aha! Clearly, I would have preferred to publish this book earlier but the fact is that things may not always go as planned and when God lets those things happen, we need to be able to live with that. In retrospect, I think it got published in its due time, and I'm thankful for all of it. All of that to say that our part is to ensure that we put in the work and use our time wisely (that really is what we can control) but we shouldn't beat ourselves up if things we can't control disrupt those plans.

2. Uncertainty

What if I fail at it? What if I'm no good at it? What if I'm unable to give the required attention to that task? Why even start? Where do I start from? How do I go about it? What if I don't get any emotional support from my loved ones? What toll will this take on my finances? Will I still be able to have that life that I always dreamed for myself if I pursue the God-path? Questions we have either asked ourselves or will at some point.

So, let's do ourselves a favour and ask these questions instead: What if I excel at it? What if I am able to give the required time and attention despite my tight schedule? What if I just start from somewhere, and work my way up there? What if God gives me His divine wisdom to tackle the challenges I meet on my way? (and He will). What if God raises people to support me along this journey? What if this does not have negative effects on my finances and if it does, what if God makes a way? What if God has bigger dreams for me than what I have for myself? (and He does).

Many times, we're so busy focusing on the impossibilities and uncertainties (we discussed fear in a previous chapter). So many questions and what-ifs running through our minds that keep us second-guessing the path that the Lord is setting our foot on. Worried about not what we are certain *will* go wrong but by what **could** go wrong.

But we forget that when we're at the center of God's will for our lives, that's the most certain place to ever be. Why is it so hard for us to believe that He has our best interests at heart and is looking out for us? The funny thing is that if we were to orchestrate our own lives, it would be an utter mess no matter how glittery it might seem at first. The flesh will always fail but the peace that comes with trusting in God is second to none. If He could give His son to save us, what else would He not give for us?

"Trust in the Lord with all your heart and lean not on your own understanding" - Proverbs 3:5, NIV

"Every word of God is pure; He is a shield to them that put their trust in Him" - Proverbs 30:5, AKJV

3. Lack of motivating company

"Whoever walks with the wise becomes wise, but the companion of fools will suffer harm" - Proverbs 13:20, ESV

Who are your friends? Who are the people that have the most impact on your life? Are they people you want to be like? Do they spur you to live a godly life? It's easy to neglect the kind of friends we keep in the name of 'I don't want to judge this person or I don't want them to feel like I'm too churchy' but we forget that these are the people that have the most impact on us. It's almost impossible for your life to not mirror those whom you let feed into your life, those you listen to the most. There's nothing wrong with praying for people from afar if we notice that they have a negative influence on our lives. If you and your friends don't talk about God and meaningful things, you might find it hard to live that life God designed for you. On the flip side, what kind of friend are you?

4. Lack of funds

Previously, we talked about finances and how to use it in the way that God intended for us. Now, we'll talk briefly about when we don't even have the money required to start an assignment God has laid on our hearts. Financial strain is one of the causes of anxiety for many people so this is a real issue. Ever felt that 'if only I had more money' feeling? Lack of funds can make things difficult. How do we fulfil purpose when we're barely putting food on our table?

Since fulfilling purpose does not necessarily equate to being wealthy, the good news is that we can actually live a fulfilling life regardless of our financial circumstances - I'm not going to say that this is easy though. Remember how we talked about the mindset of 'if the Lord hasn't given me, then I don't need it?' I should also add that if you, at any point, lack financially, let it not because you were lazy when you should have been grinding. The Lord might have previously given us opportunities to learn a skill, trade, or get some kind of degree but we didn't and now we're paying for it (and there's always grace to start over if this is the case). Other times, it could just be that we already have all we need, and we just need to dig deeper. Regardless of the circumstance, what I do know is that if the assignment is of God, He will always give us the wisdom to sort things out financially and make provision for us somehow.

Some final points to note on this topic:

i. **No gain without pain.** Living a life of purpose requires sacrifice and this sacrifice is not only that of our time. It's how we become built for more. Let's not go into the journey thinking that everything including our finances will work out as perfectly as we had pictured it. However, let's rest in the assurance that if God called us to it, He can and will see us through.

ii. **Ask the Lord for wisdom on your financial spending.** Many times, we seem to have it all financially planned out in our heads. But we forget that human plans can fail, no matter how smart and calculated.

Could it be that there are certain things we're spending on that the Lord really doesn't have a say in? When we have an attitude of 'It's my money and I can use it as I please,' we fail to recognize the fact that God gave that money to us. May we always remember that He is indeed interested in the tiniest things that concern us, including that shopping spree we went on when we shouldn't have.

iii. **Don't discount the fact that God can raise people to help you.** I have seen how God turns things around in the lives of His children. How He raises other people on their behalf, and turns the situation around when His children make their Father's business their business. Do your part and show yourself diligent to the cause that concerns your heavenly Father. Prove yourself a good steward; worthy of the assignment He called you to. And let Him do the rest.

5. Random Distractions

As you would have already noticed, we live in a noisy world and it's very easy to live a life that only does so much as goes with the flow. It's like there's a new distraction for each day - think about how much easier it is to spend hours on a video game or random movie streaming service than it is to meditate and spend time with God. How long are we going to allow things fill up our hearts and heads that we really have no use for?

And most of these tools are not evil in themselves, for example, it's interesting to see the same distracting social media being used for meaningful things. You have a ton of work to do or you haven't spoken to God the entire day but it's more convenient to grab your phone or laptop to check what random people are doing with their lives at the moment. The truth is that these distractions we've filled our lives with – to steal our attention momentarily are now becoming addictive. I understand that with the use of entertainment tools, circumstances are different; for example, we may just be taking a break to do something relaxing or going on social media to share helpful content. I definitely believe that we all need those days when we just let ourselves relax after but the problem is that most people do these at the wrong times while important things are left to suffer at the hand of our negligence.

I love that social media helps us connect with people more easily even in different time zones but sometimes, I can't help but wonder what older generations did with their time when there was no social media or internet frenzy. Perhaps they were more thoughtful than we are, perhaps they invested more in their human relationships, perhaps they read more books than we do today, perhaps they were able to be more consistent in their walk with God.

The only thing you shouldn't be able to do without is God. If you ever find yourself glorifying stuff that was meant to entertain you, in a way that it has become your actual life, becoming a god in your life, it may be a good time to take a break from that space. Go on a social media/technology fast if you've never tried this before and you'll find that you're less distracted and better able to focus on key tasks at hand.

For you, it might be the discipline to wake up every morning and not immediately grab your phone before anything else.

Studies show that the average adult picks up their phone 2617 times in a day and hey, this is just the average. Some do it as often as 4000 times. We function as though our mobile phones are an extension of our limbs.

Get off your phone - shove it somewhere for a few hours, get away from the TV, away from the noise. These things were made for man, not man for them. Try forming good human relationships instead, meditating more, spending more time praying and studying the word of God, reading books that will add value to you, going to places where you'll meet like-minds, or even seeing new places if you can. Don't let the world's distractions take away the yearning that God placed in you unlock the more He's deposited in you. Quick tip: if possible, don't take your phone to bed with you. Let your Bible be the first thing you grab in the morning instead.

Parents, we have work to do. Jean Twenge, a psychology professor at San Diego State University who writes extensively on youth and mental health, released the results of a study which showed a correlation between the rise of smartphone and increasing rate of suicidal thoughts and actual suicide among teenagers. Many youngsters feel like they have to be on social media all the time or someone might gossip about them. They're afraid that they might be left behind if they're not on there to get the latest gist. They feel pressured that they don't look as hot as their classmate who gets a million likes when she posts her photos on the gram. How did we get here?

We can redefine these things for our children. Let's raise children that can pick up books when they are bored instead of electronic gadgets (I know this is hard, it's a struggle in our house - because even we the parents use electronic gadgets for almost everything). I know there are times when this is completely unavoidable, but let's not give up trying. And here's the twist: The only way kids pick up stuff is when they see people around them do it. You can yell all you want about their excessive screen time but if you're doing the same thing as a parent, it's pretty much pointless. Whenever I'm reading a book and my son says, *'Mommy, I wan' read wi-yu,'* I feel like I'm doing something right. Kids do what we do, not what we say, so, it definitely starts with us. We have a responsibility to show them that life does not have to be the way the world portrays it.

Aside from social media and entertainment, there are many other things that could be distracting us from fulfilling purpose. It could be a relationship, the general state of our minds, or the fact that we're just busy chasing the wrong things. You might be in a relationship you know you have no business being in. You might be in a relationship that only draws you away from God at best. Quick assessment: Can I serve God with this person I'm in a relationship with? Will this relationship draw me closer to God or farther from Him?

Sometimes, the issue is that our minds are just clogged with unhealthy emotions like envy and malice. It is impossible for us to truly love and care about other people when we are bitter. To fulfil purpose, we have to notice that there's a void in our hearts but we won't notice this void if our hearts are already filled with hatred, jealousy, or anger. We also can't live our best possible lives if we don't have love in our hearts. Purpose is fulfilled out of love for God and humanity so naturally, this will be difficult when we have zero love in our hearts. If you find that your intentions towards other people are bad, it's time for some re-evaluation and renewal of your mind.

"Dear friends, let us love one another, for love comes from God. Everyone who loves has been born of God and knows God. Whoever does not love does not know God, because God is love" - 1 John 4:7-8, NIV

This scripture doesn't mean that we're not allowed to express our anger or disapproval towards something or someone. It is not a sin to be angry – in fact, scriptures tell us that it is okay to be angry, only that we should not sin in the midst of our anger. Anger is a normal human emotion that we're allowed to feel but we are to deal with that feeling of anger appropriately, and not let it overcome us. Some people say things they don't mean when they're angry. If you're prone to saying hurtful things when you're angry, learn to excuse yourself before things get heated.

Another thing that could distract us from fulfilling purpose is when we're chasing after every other thing except God. You may find that you're just busy trying to create a name for yourself when God has already called you by His name, or you're just striving for fame. Don't forget that not all famous people are necessarily fulfilled. Many of us will fulfil purpose by just serving faithfully in the back scenes where only God rewards. The fact that it isn't publicized doesn't mean that it isn't done.

What is causing you to be distracted today? It remains your responsibility, and mine to ensure that we do our best to live the lives God purposed for us. Remember, the goal is to as much as we can, fulfil the calling of God upon our lives in whatever situation we're in - not just when we have the perfect situation.

6. Ill health

Honestly, there's not much that can be done when you're down with sickness. But even if it's a word of prayer we could manage to say in those moments, it counts for something in its own way. Few months before this book was published, I was in a rough phase – it wasn't exactly due to ill health but I'd never had so many medical appointments, blood work, or medication in such little space of time. Last thing on my mind was how to publish a book. Many of us have had those moments when we felt like we couldn't achieve anything because we were down but then we got healed eventually, praise the Lord. What surprises me though is that when we bounce back to life, we still hardly do those things we wished we could have been able to do when we were ill.

Let's always make use of life and good health when we're privileged to have it. Let's ensure that we're making hay while the sun shines. Let's make use of the days when we're strong, agile and in good health. Just like death, illnesses and accidents never really give us a fair notice. They can happen to anyone at any time. If you're in good health, please make the best of it: fulfil purpose, live for God.

If you're reading this and you're down with an ailment, or know a loved one who is, do not despair. God is able to revive that body and bring it back to full vitality. Keep trusting Him, keep praising Him. I know that it might be tough but I also know that God knows our pain and sees our troubles. We're not alone; never have been, never will be. And there is purpose in our pain.

IX

How You Know You're Fulfilling Purpose

"Brothers and sisters, I do not consider myself yet to have taken hold of it. But one thing I do: Forgetting what is behind and straining toward what is ahead"

— Philippians 3:13, NIV

As we move closer to the end of this book, I'd like to spend this chapter looking at some pointers or ways that we know we're at the center of God's will for our lives.

1. You can sense it

There's not much to be said here. When you no longer have that nagging feeling that a major piece of your life is missing and you don't feel empty or guilty for not living in the fullness of your God-given potential, you've probably begun to live in your purpose.

What is the witness in your spirit saying? Do you have some catching up to do? Do you sense that you're in a good place spiritually? When you're fulfilling purpose, you tend to feel more vibrant and you find it easier to come alive. That being said, we should never get to a point where we feel like we have 'arrived'. As long as we're still breathing, there's always something more - God always wants to take us deeper and closer.

If your situation is the opposite, don't be discouraged about where you are right now as opposed to where you could or should have been. Instead, continue to push in the direction God is guiding you each day. Be truthful to yourself but also forgive yourself, I mean why be hard on yourself when God has already forgiven you? Give yourself grace and time to develop and grow. And when you begin to attain that maturity, you'll just know.

You may not be where God wants you to be yet but you can and will get there. When you are living in purpose, you're confident that you are doing the right thing and you only want to do more of it. You still have questions (we all do and I'm sure we'll have all the answers when we get to heaven), but you know you're on the right track in your life. There's no confusion when you're fulfilling purpose, rather there's an inner conviction and confirmation.

Have you heeded God's voice or are you still trying to create a hodgepodge of 'my way' and 'God's-way'? You can't be in the middle. Surrendering to God is daily practice. It starts with the little things - the same ones we've talked about the entire time. When we have a habit of surrendering to Him in the little things daily, we won't find it difficult to surrender our big scenes to Him. And when we do, our lives become more meaningful. Everything begins to make sense: our past, our experiences, our circumstances, our passions, and of course, our purpose.

I like to use the term 'purpose journey' because fulfilling purpose is not supposed to be a one-time thing. We don't just do one thing and then we're done fulfilling purpose. As long as we are breathing, we're not done. It's a journey that would last our entire lives. And we were never meant to go through this journey alone. We were meant to walk with Him and let Him guide us through it all.

> *"Teach these new disciples to obey all the commands I have given you. And be sure of this: I am with you always, even to the end of the age" - Matthew 28:20, NLT*

How do you feel when you see other people living the life God called them to live? Do you feel like they have come again and 'their own is too much'? Or are you genuinely happy to see these people living out their purpose? Are they a reminder that you need to be doing more? Because that's a good thing. It's good pressure when it's filled with inspiration and not envy.

2. You personally feel fulfilled

The Cambridge Dictionary defines fulfilment as a feeling of happiness that comes when you are doing what you intended to do with your life. Fulfilment is that deep satisfaction that comes from accomplishing a goal or objective. If we have understood the gist of this book by now, fulfilment means the joy that comes from knowing one is achieving purpose in life. True fulfilment is only derived from having a relationship with God and fulfilling purpose in life. We can only be truly fulfilled when we're living the life that God called us to live.

It's good to achieve collective goals (goals of a body or organisation that you belong to) but nothing beats personal goals' achievement and personal fulfilment. I've found that it's easier to pour into others when you're already feeling fulfilled. Empty will always pour nothing, but a full cup can always pour its contents into another cup. We have to decide if we'll be full cups or empty cups.

When we're not fulfilled, we're likely to be easily disgruntled, irritable and less understanding of other people's situations. But when we are fulfilled, being thankful for the little things comes naturally to us. Fulfilment wells up a spring of thanksgiving and gratefulness from within us. Fulfilment can't be bought or sold. It is the result of some kind of achievement, and it is usually related to our life dreams and aspirations.

Of course, we can be fulfilled in several aspects of our lives but the most important is when we're fulfilled because we are living for God daily. When you're fulfilled, you find that you're not struggling to gain anyone's approval. Because you're more occupied with living your life as passionately for God as you can. With godly fulfilment, you no longer feel like you are hiding a part of what makes you 'you'. You become so real and true to yourself that you can tell yourself even the hardest truths.

Godly fulfilment is borne out of consciousness and intention. Consciousness to set godly goals, recognize God's hand at work in the storm, and to recognize answered prayers even when they don't look like what we envisaged. Godly fulfilment brings about joy – one derived from bringing others joy because it truly cares about other people.

3. You are impacting lives positively

Every single day of our lives, we're impacting the people around us one way or the other. You don't even have to be an 'influencer' to do this. And when we think of impact, we don't even ned to think too deep about it. Impact simply means marked effect or influence. We have more impact than we think we do, and we don't even have to go out of our way before we impact other people. Sociologists say the most introverted person will influence at least ten thousand other people in their lifetime. Think about the number of people you've ever met and intentionally or unintentionally influenced so far.

The average life expectancy ratio is around 70 years worldwide. Most of us only remember the people we meet after 5 years old, but let's conservatively peg it at 18 years since that's when we more or less become adults. So, that's about 52 years of possible impact (70 - 18 years). You follow me? Say you meet one new person daily for 52 years (this could definitely be more or less), that is 52 years X 1 new person X 365 days a year = 18,980 people. That's around the number of people you will have some kind of impact on (or may have already impacted, depending on your age). Don't take your everyday human contacts for granted.

Impact could be minimal or massive, it could be positive or negative. And as long as we come in contact with other people from time to time, we're impacting them one way or the other. The big question is: how do/will we impact them? Are we going to leave a bad taste in the mouth of the people who come in contact with us or are we a delight to them?

It's in the little things: the emails, phone calls, face to face interaction, online interactions. If you compliment a co-worker on their performance on a task, you've had some kind of impact on that person. If you criticize someone harshly, you've also impacted them. If you help an elderly person hold the door out, you've impacted them. Whether or not they say thank you, will impact you in some form too. Is it not sad that most of the effect we will have on people will not be intentional or calculated? Maybe the world would be a better place if we really thought about how the other person would feel when we do or say something to them?

Your impact defines your reality and your reality becomes your legacy. You can make more impact than you think and you have the ability to define the kind of impact you will make in life. Don't underestimate your influence. The moment you wake up in the morning and remember that you have a choice to decide what kind of impact it will be that day, you'll be more intentional about your life. Is your attitude going to encourage people to do better or are you going to discourage them before you even speak a word to them? When you live each day intentionally, there's no limit to what you can achieve. Are you adding value to the lives of people around you or are you just taking up space?

Purpose is not selfish, solipsistic or self-centred. It cares about the impact that our actions have on other people since other people will come to be affected by whether we fulfil purpose or not. When we're living in purpose, the feeling of 'what people will think' about our calling will be replaced with the feeling of knowing that the world actually needs us to take our place.

4. Other people can testify to it

"You are the light of the world. A city set on a hill cannot be hidden" - Matthew 5:14, ESV

The reason a city set on a hill cannot be hidden is because it is in a visible spot, and so everyone can see it from afar. You don't even have to move too close to see it. This is how you are when God's light is shining through and in you for the world to see. It becomes clear no matter how much you try to hide it. Your light was never meant to be hidden under a shed. God needs you to sparkle.

Do you realize that you are one of God's stars? He placed you on earth to shine. He placed you here to fulfil purpose. He placed you here to reflect His love and His light; not for you to go into hiding. Where does your star currently live? Is it chilling inside the clouds or is it visible like it should be? Have you gone undercover because of the trying times you've had in life?

I'm no physics expert, but in astronomy, it is said that young stars derive their energy from gravity (gravity is one of the four fundamental forces of physics and the process by which all things with mass or energy are brought towards one another). These stars are slowly contracting (like what happens when we go through hard times), and as they squeeze together (which is why we shouldn't be doing life alone), this generates energy and the energy gets radiated away as light. Whenever I remember this, I go *Wow*.

The closest star to the earth is called the 'Proxima Centauri' and is believed to be 4.24 light-years away. To put this in perspective, one light-year is 9.44 trillion kilometres or 5.88 trillion miles. Again, this star is the closest star to the earth so you can only imagine how bright it is, for it to be visible to us. It reminds me of the journey of life. Our challenges make us stronger and with the right support, the light of God will shine brightly through us.

X

The cost of not Living Purposefully

It is my prayer that by now, you have a better idea of the concept of fulfilling purpose, of being all that God called you to do. What really is the cost of not living life to its fullest potential?

1. You forfeit your joy

> *"For the kingdom of God is not a matter of eating and drinking but of righteousness and peace and joy in the Holy Spirit." - Romans 4:17, NIV*

I dare say that the main beneficiary when you're living your calling is actually you. It may seem like other people are the receivers of your light. And that's true but actually, you're the one who benefits the most from your purpose journey. Nobody else gets that fulfilment or joy that comes with living your life in service to God.

Happiness and joy are typically used interchangeably but there's a difference between both. Happiness is an emotion that ranges from various phenomena like satisfaction, bliss, and pleasure. Joy is beyond just an emotion - it is the state of your mind; the condition of your soul. Joy is much less common in the world than happiness and it is achieved when we're spiritually connected to God. The difference between happiness and joy is God.

When we talk about happiness, the things that make you happy can make you sad, even the people in your life. It is great to be happy, we all long to be happy and there's nothing wrong with that - I love to be happy. God wants us to be happy. However, beyond happiness, He intended for us to have everlasting joy. We put so much pressure on the blessings (people and material things) in our lives and this is why it's easy for us to sink into sadness when the 'blessings' that used to make us happy are not making us happy in a particular moment.

There's a song by Sheryl Crow titled 'If It Makes You Happy' and this is how the chorus goes: 'If it makes you happy, it can't be that bad. If it makes you happy, then why the hell are you so sad?' Really, does it not just make sense to NOT feel sad when you have something makes you happy? Isn't this the expected? Why will you be sad when you should be happy by the world's standards? Why do we have sad billionaires, sad couples (even though they have great marriages), sad comedians (though they tell jokes that make us happy), sad career people (even though they have great jobs)? And then, we think in our minds: 'Why is this person sad, she seems to have the perfect life.' But guess what? You and I are these people too.

The answer is simple. There's a void in every human heart

that only God can fill. He intentionally put this emptiness, this hollow in us as a reminder that we still have to make recourse to Him, as a reminder that we should not be so dependent on the blessings He has given us. He wants us to come to Him for that everlasting joy that we so direly need. One that has no strings attached, that is unconditional, that is not a function of how smart we are, that remains with us even when nothing else is working in our lives, that we have obtained freely by virtue of being His sons and daughters. This joy is a fruit of His Spirit.

Because He loves us unconditionally, He gives us this joy unconditionally. Think of happiness as mercurial, but the joy of the Lord as stable and consistent. Happiness is based on events that **have occurred** but the joy of the Lord is based on events that have not only occurred but also that **will occur**. Happiness is as a result of something that happened to us for example, we got a new car. Joy is as a result of both something that happened to us (the redemptive work of Christ) and something that will happen to us (reigning with Him forever in eternity).

The joy of the Lord is derived from an understanding of His promises and the hope of what is to come. The joy of the Lord comes from fellowshipping with His Holy Spirit. Although sometimes I fall short, I'm learning to constantly fill that void with God's word as against filling it with the other things happening in my life.

Quite often, we say 'I just want to be happy'. However, I think it's time to shift base from merely just wanting to be happy. It is time to understand that we're not called to a life of being 'just happy' or cute. We are called to something much deeper than that. We are not called to just get by in life; it's something better than that. The time is right for us to seek the real joy and peace in Christ and share same to others. If all of our efforts are focused on just trying to be happy, we don't really need Jesus.

However, if our efforts are directed at having joy in our lives then we automatically commit to something better than just self-satisfaction. This is what fulfilling purpose opens your eyes to see and your hands to do. Joy is derived from living our lives for God and serving the people He has called us to serve without expecting anything in return. Joy is found in the love of God, and in loving others with the love of God. Joy is found in bringing others joy.

I think of the sequence like this: When we know the Lord, have a deep understanding of His promises, and consistently renew our minds with His word, we have joy. When we have joy, we naturally want to spread it to other people and this is how we fulfil purpose. When we're fulfilling our God-given assignments and making a positive impact in people's lives, we bring them joy. And when we bring them joy, we derive joy again.

"If you keep my commands, you will remain in my love, just as I have kept my Father's commands and remain in His love. I have told you this so that my joy may be in you and that your joy may be complete." - John 15:10-11, NIV

2. You fail the world

I tried to see if I could put this mildly but I couldn't. Only when God's people heed His call can He do the great and mighty things that He wants to do amongst us. We are God's hands here on earth called to bring heaven to earth and manifest His works on earth. When we don't use the talents that God deposited in us, we ignore our individual assignments. And when we ignore our individual assignments, we won't bask in the fullness of God's purpose for our lives.

The interesting thing is that God's assignment will be done irrespective of whether we choose to make ourselves available or not. He will always use willing vessels; whether that's you and me, or not. He won't beg any vessel to be useful, He raises others. Do you remember how the one talent given to the proud fellow who neither used nor invested it, was eventually added to that of the guy with ten talents?

<u>We are the clay, He the potter</u>

Pottery is one of the oldest human inventions. It is said to have originated before the Neolithic period or the new stone-age. Pottery is the process of forming a body of ceramic or clay into objects of a preferred shape and heating them to high temperatures in a kiln which removes all the water from the clay. This in turn induces reactions that lead to permanent changes including increasing their strength, hardening and setting their shape.

Pottery is one of those analogies used in scripture to depict

God's creation (you and me) in relation to Him. The pottery is nothing without the potter. Without the potter, the pottery won't be the pottery that it is. If we truly understand this, then we wouldn't be okay with just living life on our own terms. Are we letting God mould us into who He wants us to be or are we trying to mould ourselves?

> *"Woe to those who quarrel with their Maker, those who are nothing but potsherds among the potsherds on the ground. Does the clay say to the potter, 'What are you making?' Does your work say, 'The potter has no hands'?"*
> *- Isaiah 45:9, NIV*

Let's yield ourselves totally to our creator. Let's make ourselves available for the people whose lives we need to touch. Not because it will add anything to God but because it will add to us. God will use somebody else if we don't yield to Him but it's a privilege for Him to give us assignments; for Him to have His eyes on us, and count on us.

3. You fail God and miss out on your rewards.

> *"Their work will be shown for what it is, because the day will bring it to light. It will be revealed with fire, and the fire will test the quality of each person's work. If what has been built survives, the builder will receive a reward. If it is burned up, the builder will suffer loss but yet will be saved—even though only as one escaping through the flames" - 1 Corinthians 3:13 – 15, NIV*

And this scripture resurfaces again. If you ever wondered: *what really is in it for serving God or what is my gain in all of this, am I only to sacrifice it all?* There are rewards both on earth and in heaven for our works whether good or bad. Scriptures says that for every one of us, all of our works will be tested. The narrative that we will all give account of how we lived our life to God will never get old.

There will come a day when we will have done our time here on earth and all that will be left is to submit our works at the feet of the father for 'verification'. You won't be asked how many followers you had on social media, you will be asked how you spent your life. You will be asked if you lived your life for God. You will be asked what you did with your talent and the influence that you had. You will give account not because the heavens do not already know but because there is something about giving one's account by oneself. As long as you are saved, you won't be denied entry into heaven if you didn't fulfil purpose (refer to the last sentence in the above scripture). However, that will be all there is to you on that day of judgement. Why have less when you can have more?

Because God is a rewarder of those who diligently seek Him, He never forgets our labor of love. He is not an unfair or unjust God and none of our toil is in vain. I have witnessed first hand (how He rewards us, even here on earth) and it's hard to explain. No one sees your pain like Him, no one knows how much you sacrifice your comfort for Him like Him; no one. Some things happen to me in life and I just sense God casting my mind back to certain days when I served Him in the face of persecution. For a fact, He is a great rewarder of those who diligently seek Him.

If you're currently in a season where it looks like you've sacrificed everything possible for Him, know that this is the best position you can ever possibly be in. He sees it all and He never forgets. He will reward you in due time and when His reward comes, you'll just know.

XI

Let's Wrap this Up, Shall We?

Ah we're at the end! I included this final chapter to discuss general principles I've learnt so far in this ongoing journey of life.

1. Prepare your mind for unexpected things

One would have thought that nine or ten months were enough time to prepare the mind of prospective parents for what lies ahead. I mean, the moment the pee-on-the-stick-result turns out positive, you already know that you're going to be a mommy or a daddy, if no glitches occur during the pregnancy. However, I am now resigning to the conclusion that nothing can adequately prepare anyone for parenthood. As the days, weeks, months and years go by, you begin to discover the peculiarity of your child(ren), understand their character and how to relate with them.

I was not particularly new to handling babies as I was very much around my big sister when she had her first two babies.

While I was not new to diaper changing and baby feeding, I clearly didn't have a complete grasp of what parenthood really entailed until I was in it. The first shock for me was the sleepless nights and breastfeeding issues I faced during the first few weeks. I literally felt like I was never going to be able to get a good night's sleep ever again. Then the sleepless nights reduced, as did the breastfeeding problems of our first few weeks (yaay!). And then when my baby clocked nine months, I had that vasospasm (a word which I never knew existed until it happened to me) condition I talked about earlier, and breastfeeding once again became a nightmare.

As my baby began to become more mentally aware and active, it dawned on me that things were changing and he was not always going to be my innocent little bub. I quickly realized that raising a child was more than sloppy kisses and cuddles (two of my favorite activities). Raising a child entails introducing them to the differences between right and wrong. It entails teaching them about patience, love and respect for other people. It entails guiding them with towards ensuring that they grow into well rounded and well-behaved citizens of the world. It entails loving them like nobody's business, introducing them to the way of God and praying for them. It entails re-affirming them and holding their hands to get through their most embarrassing moments. Oh, and did I mention the bills that come with having a child?

Needless to say, the journey isn't easy-peasy; it's filled with a lot of discoveries and unexpected happenings. Once they discover their own personality, we begin to notice different traits. As we dialogue with them, they share a little of what goes on in their little minds; many of which will be surprising to us.

Our lives don't end at discovering our purpose; this is in fact the starting point and a lot more water will pass under the bridge. It pays to have a mind-set that is prepared for a ride of uncertainties, similar to this one with parenthood. Like defensive driving, anticipate other people's errors, and be aware that things you didn't plan for will happen. I am a planner and it irks me when things don't go according to my plan but hello, world.

On your purpose journey, you may discover that some of your loved ones don't really support you, and you find the most unexpected people supporting you on this beautiful journey. People will surprise you (and this might be a little harder to accommodate, if you're sensitive or emotional) but you need to develop a thick skin, to not take offence when the surprise is unpleasant. One the other hand, some people just need time to believe in your dreams with you, and I find that this is very common with many humans. We want to see how much that person is really invested in their own dreams, before we invest our emotions and time into their dreams. People want to see you believe in your own dreams first, they need to see how passionate you are about them before they can believe in it with you. So, if the people you expected to support you are not doing so right now, it's okay. Keep doing what the Lord has called you to do. With time, some of them will come around. Others may not but either ways, God's got you.

Apart from surprises, prepare your mind for inconveniences because they will happen. You'll face trials, temptations and rough days but He will be with you through it all. God may ask you to deliver uncomfortable messages, He might send you to places that you do not want to go, but I think it's best to go. This is by no means a threat but I can't help but remember Jonah, his assignment to the people of Nineveh and how he ended up in the belly of the fish. God will position you according to a higher priority and not your preferences. As a result, you may have to do things that you never knew you could do. Ask Abraham, Moses, and Paul.

God will position you for your assignment but He won't take the step for you. That would be dictatorship and it's not how He operates because we still have a choice in all of this. Fulfilling purpose and doing the will of God is simple, not easy. If you say you're surrendered to God, you have to be surrendered in your thoughts and deeds too.

You may also have days when you don't just feel like getting out of bed. Perhaps you're just faced with all sorts of challenges. It may seem like the doors are being shut in your face, even though you thought they were doors that God opened. You may be physically tired or needing motivation. On days like this, your best bet is to catch some rest if this is what it takes for you to be re-motivated (you're not trying to prove a point to anybody). Then feed on the word of God, spend sometime in the place of prayer, fellowship with the Holy Spirit, and surround yourself with godly people.

Remember why you started in the first place - why you made up your mind that you would fulfil purpose, that you would do anything that He needed you to do and go anywhere He needed you to go. Remember where He brought you from. Remember how you cannot afford to go back to the things He saved you from, how He saved you from yourself.

2. Not everything you like is your purpose

My dear husband is one of the most brilliant people I know and I am blessed that I get to do life with him. However, the love of my life cannot sing, although he does make an absolutely great music producer. I could ask him to sing along with me while I'm singing a song and I'll give him his part to sing. Apart from the fact that we'll have to go over his part ninety-nine times, he'll keep hopping into my soprano or alto part once we start to sing together. Funniest part is that he likes to sing.

It's not every assignment around us that God has automatically called us to. As a consequence, it's not everything we like that we need to pursue vehemently. I like horseback riding but I cannot partake in it except when it's for a few minutes at the beach and there are about twenty guides there with me. There's absolutely no need to be ashamed when you're not talented in a certain area, find your own area of talent – I can assure you it's there.

3. Give yourself room to make new friends and valuable relationships

In the previous chapter, I talked about the young stars in the galaxy and how the pressure of gravity makes them stick together and how this energy produces the light that we see from earth. Like the saying, no man is an island, it's always good to have like-minded people in your life who understand what you're doing and support you on your journey.

God designed us to need other people. Not because we

cannot function on our own but because support is good. To pray for you and hold your hands during rough days. God can and will orchestrate valuable relationships in your life for you to achieve your assignment. But your eyes and ears have to be open to notice these people when He places them in your way.

You never know where you'll meet people or how but friendships are usually not pre-planned; they grow over time. You won't have the privilege of new valuable relationships if you are surly or focused on yourself alone. Be cautious of character traits, but keep an open mind when meeting and dealing with people; you just never know.

On the flip side (and I know we touched on this earlier), everyone is not supposed to be your friend. Since people rub off on us and vice-versa, it's likely that eventually, we will begin to manifest the thinking and behaviours of our closest friends. Therefore, we want to carefully select our closest friends.

Acquaint yourself with the people that you want to be like. If you want to grow spiritually, your best friends should be people who desire this as well. God will place people along your path who will help you get to where you are going but you have to be in position, listen to His instructions and follow those instructions. People are God's hands on earth. On one hand, God will use you to help some individuals while on the other hand, God will raise some people to support you as well. Therefore, you will find two different types of people that will come into your life. One, those that you have the ability to help, and two, those who have the ability to help you. Recognizing these two kinds of people is vital. When we have relationships, we should know how to leverage them by asking for help when we need it. Asking for help doesn't make you any less of yourself. When I first started writing, I did not realize how much redundancies were in my writing until my husband started to occasionally review and editi my articles for me.

4. Your purpose journey does not have to replicate someone else's

It's so easy for us to map our lives along the lines and patterns of an individual that we look up to but we should be careful with doing this. Say we set out on the assignment or job we think we're called to and we have an idea of what it should be like, more so we know at least one person who started just like us and whose calling is just like ours. Is it not safe to assume that we will face the same mountains that they faced and enjoy the same victories they did? It is not. Your purpose journey is specific to you, own it. It may seem like it but there's really no expected pattern that your life is supposed to follow. The only pattern you need and have is the word of God.

5. Celebrate your small wins

Yes! How do you want to celebrate your big wins if you can't rejoice in your small wins? Yes, eyes on the prize; eyes on the bigger picture but life is in phases and each stage must be celebrated. How do I celebrate small wins? You may ask. Start by celebrating those little goals that you meet. For every time you meet up with your goal or surpass your target, reward yourself. It is up to you to decide how to reward yourself and in advance, you can list your potential rewards alongside your goals. It doesn't matter how old you are, or if other people typically achieve that feat at a younger age. You are unique. Celebrate you!

6. Make use of your opportunities

Someone once said: *'Talents are many, it is opportunities that are scarce.'* However scarce opportunities may be though, they are still around. How well are you making use of your opportunities? And not all opportunities that come your way need to be seized by you, we must judge all opportunities with the word of God. Before that, there are ways you could create opportunities for yourself and for others (see some ideas below). And you have what it takes.

i. **<u>Open your heart, eyes and ears.</u>** If you will be a creator of opportunities, your eyes and heart will need to be opened. You will need to begin to look at things differently from the way you'd normally see them. Opportunities are born where there is a need, and the ability to proffer a solution to a problem. You will not be able to provide a solution if you are unable to identify a need. And identifying needs happens when you use your *conscious* more often in your daily life than you do your *sub-conscious*.

This is the part where you ask questions. Have you seen how three and four-year olds question everything? They will test your patience, especially when you're the one to provide the answers. When my niece was around that age, she'd ask questions like: my aunty, why is this chair black, who is that person that grandma greeted on the road, why did you say my mummy *should-don't-worry* yesterday, why did you do your hand like this? And when I say: 'I don't know', I get the mother of all questions, 'My aunty, *why-did-you-not-know?*' Sigh. Funny as it sounds, we have one or two things to learn from children.

There comes a time in everyone's life when they question the very things they've always believed. And when this time comes, it's perfectly alright, even if it has to do with your faith. Doubt is not the same as unbelief. Throw away the biases and just learn. You cannot learn or grow if you don't ask questions. In the capacity to think deep and ask relevant questions is the ability to see a gap and provide solutions.

ii. **<u>Make good use of your relationships.</u>** For someone who has spent a number of years in the professional world, I've seen how a simple referral can change a person's life. Of course, don't be that person who just wants to take advantage of their relationships, adding no real value to the other person. When you are seen as someone who just needs 'connections', you may turn the other person off; today it's 'please connect me with the CEO of XXX', tomorrow it's 'I heard you know the MD of YYYY'. If the only reason you ever get in touch with a friend is because you need them to connect you to another person, I think you'll quickly come across as annoying.

Breaking out of your comfort zone might include going out of your way to meet people. Attend conferences, workshops, programmes that add value to you if you're led to do so, and God will bring people along your path that will help you get to the promised land.

iii. **<u>Be ready for change.</u>** Although I don't agree that change is the only constant in life, change is indeed constant. We all hear and know this, yet we find it difficult to adapt when change comes. Why? We humans do not like anything that will take us out of our comfort zone. Unfortunately, out of our comfort zone is where all the goodies are. If you're looking to be a creator of opportunities, then certain things will have to change. And you need to be ready for when they do.

7. Not all opportunities are meant to be taken

I like that this point immediately follows the above point. Remember that scripture that says: *'All things are lawful (permissible) but not all things are expedient (beneficial or profitable)'.* So how do we know when to make use of an opportunity? Here are a few ways that work for me; I call this the three-fold test, and for me, this applies in my general decision-making. One, ask yourself if the opportunity is in accordance with your personal convictions and beliefs (based on the word of God). For example, if the opportunity will get you to fall into something that you consider sinful or get you to commit an offence, you want to rethink it. You'll know which opportunity is meant for you when you stay connected to God.

Two, is your spirit at peace with the idea of this opportunity? And I am not talking about the initial euphoria that hits you when you first realize that that window of opportunity exists. The prospects may appear very exciting but it will do you some good if you don't make the decision in haste. I find that things appear clearer when I sleep over them and pray about them before making a final decision as to what to do. As a matter of fact, be wary of opportunities that give you no time to consider whether you want to seize them or not.

Three, when in doubt consult your confidant; that person that you trust, can talk to, has your best interest at heart, and will give you godly counsel, ask them what they think.

8. Take a break when you need it

I say this to myself too and I know that I talked about rest in an earlier chapter. There is a tendency for us to want to go on a spree or overdrive when we've discovered our passion but sometimes, we get tired, and that's okay. We're humans and not vehicles to be continually pushed around in continuum.

Give yourself a break, clear your head, declutter your mind. Take a brief moment to forget about your to-dos and everything that you want to achieve. Everyone needs a consistent break time no matter how superb they are. Taking breaks help you feel more refreshed to continue in your pursuit later. You need to renew your strength from time to time. Prioritize this. And never forget that you can take a break to catch your breath but not a break from Jesus.

9. Be visible to the people that need you (your audience)

This is not the same thing as show-off, far from it. If we have been talking about making impact and touching lives, I'd think that it only makes sense to be visible to the people you feel sent to. I know you're shy but if the Lord leads you to go to a place, go there. If He leads you to accept that speaking engagement, accept it. If He leads you to give a word of encouragement or knowledge to a random person (and I know how weird this can be), give it. The fulfilment of purpose is hinged on our obedience to the spirit of God. Don't hide your calling to fit in with the world.

10. Give yourself room to keep figuring things out

I hope that you never feel pressured into thinking you need to have it all figured out at once. Don't be so hard on yourself. Nobody is the know-it-all; we will keep learning till we draw our last breaths. And if this is so, we should make an allowance to continue learning and unravelling the many different aspects of purpose that the Lord is showing us.

Maybe an idea was impressed on your heart and then you took the necessary action required at that moment and then later, you got a new assignment. Do it by all means, as long as you believe God is leading you to do it. Don't put yourself in a box or confine yourself to a particular space; do not set restrictions that God never intended for you. Go out there and do ALL of what you were made for. Be everything you were made for.

11. Forgive yourself when you make in mistakes.

We've all had that one thing we wish we never did or said, or a place we wish we never went. It's all part of life. I could tell you that from the moment you start walking with God, you will never make any mistake again in your life but that would be a lie. And our mistakes don't mean that God is not guiding us; He is willing to guide us to the extent that we allow Him. And there are times when we'll still stubbornly (or sometimes, even innocently) go our own way.

I am one to beat myself up when I make mistakes but I've come to realize that I'm not perfect and nobody is. It's good to know that God does not require us to be perfect, only for us to keep striving to walk with Him because this will save us a lot of trouble. But here's how to grace yourself when you fall short:

i. **<u>Point out what caused you to make the mistake.</u>** Not because you want to dwell on it but in order to prevent such occurrences in future. It could be lack of attention to detail, it could be a split second of forgetting your morals, it could be bad company, it could be lack of consistency, it could be almost anything. Identify the cause and you can address the issue. Don't let your mistakes get the better of you by occurring twice or more times.

That being said, don't spend a bulk of your time trying to identify what went wrong. If you cannot find what went wrong, it may have not been your mistake (sometimes, you really did the best you could, given the circumstances) and this is the part where you move on. You'd be making a bigger mistake in your present by dwelling on the past the entire time.

ii. **Be clear on your values and what you stand for.** If you ever make the kind of mistake where you contradict what you stand for or somehow portray yourself as someone you're not, this is the point where you try to become clearer on your values and remind yourself of the things that you stand for as an individual. What are your morals, what are your values, what are your convictions? This is the time to remind yourself of what the word of God says about who you are and should strive to be. Keeping His word in our hearts is the only way we won't keep falling into sin or error.

iii. **Realize that the past is in the past.** Face it, the mistake happened. Could you have done better? Maybe. But again, it is time to move on. This mistake may have cost you. It will make you sad but as long as there is nothing that you can do about it, focus on your present. Let it go. Forgive yourself. If God can forgive our mistakes time and time again, who are we to not forgive ourselves?

iv. **Love yourself.** You are better than your mistakes. Love yourself enough to make good choices. When you love yourself, you'll tell yourself the truth even when it's hard. The most dangerous lies are the ones you tell yourself; self-deceit. Love yourself enough to be brutally honest with yourself. Admit it when you fall short, and apologize to anyone you've hurt. Don't put yourself in situations that are harmful to your values convincing yourself that you can handle it.

An easy test to know whether you are doing the right thing or not is: Can it be done in the open? Can you tell your family and loved ones about it? If your answer to both questions is 'no', you're likely doing something you won't be proud of tomorrow. Living in sin is one of the easiest ways to not fulfil purpose. We can't afford to go our own way in this life – our flesh is weak.

12. Be empathetic towards people

It's easy to be the judge in other people's situations. It's easy when you are at the giving end. But it's important to put yourself in other people's shoes. Before giving up on people and before sending them off to hell in your mind, be empathetic with their situation. You may have been brought up with a silver spoon, but it would be wrong to look down on the less privileged. You may be happily married but this gives you no permission to look down on single or divorced parents.

No one is asking you to lower your standards but if you're going to learn to love like Christ, it must be from the heart.

You honestly don't know how people got into the situations they're in, but the fact that you're not in their situation doesn't make you any better than them. God loves everyone and that's why He paid the ultimate sacrifice for everyone in the world; not only a select few. To fill a need, you'll need to be more empathetic towards people than apathetic.

You are not mandated to agree with everyone; especially if their point of view is not in line with what you believe the word of God says. But you are required to live at peace with everyone as much as it is within your power. To be empathetic, you have to learn to listen to other people. Ask people if they need your advice before you proffer it; sometimes all people want is just someone to listen, someone they can pour their hearts out to. Don't be tempted to offer advice when it's not needed.

Don't try to water down someone's concerns because you have *been-there-done-that*. Even if you have, this person is at a different stage in their own life. The best you can do is to listen and answer the questions you're asked. If you then get positive confirmation that your advice is needed, you can bring up your own experience.

13. Maximize your time

I get how hard this is especially when you are a mum who'll be grateful for five minutes to brush her hair. How come it is when I need to concentrate or think that the little human in my house decides to cling to the hem of my garment? Three quarter of the time I spent writing this book, I had to deal with his little tail hanging onto me, thus making me an expert in one-handed activities like typing with one hand while I hold him on the other or stirring a pot of soup with one hand and holding him on the other. Would I have preferred it any other way though? No. Motherhood is the best job I've ever had.

Most of the time, we're only likely to get busier in life and not less-busier – for real, even if what you're doing is not productive, you can grow busy doing 'nothing'. Good things are time demanding so if you want to achieve a good thing, you'll need to devote adequate time to it despite your busy schedule.

For everyone who wants to maximize their time and honestly their life, the best way is to prioritize your activities, own your day, and structure how you want that day to go. I assure you that as long as you are reading this book right now, you are able to make the time required to lead a fulfilling life. Are you spending your time efficiently? Are you satisfied with the way that you spend your time?

It might also help to maintain a time log of how you spend your time every day for a week or more. By doing this, you are able to assess where the bulk of your time currently goes to (this will most likely be your job, business, school or home). If you are happy with the way your time is being currently spent, good for you. If you're not, you need to begin to work in those preferred activities into your schedule. If possible, don't waste your commute time. Listen to something edifying if you can do so while driving. If you're not driving, read a book on something you've been wanting to learn, or listen to an audio book. You'll be surprised at how much time you can spend better just by being intentional with your time.

14. Be patient

Sometimes when we pray, the answer is not a 'yes' or a 'no', the answer is a 'wait' for reasons best known to the Father. Answers like this teach us to be patient, if we're going to rely on Him and not go around cutting corners on our own. You must learn to wait for God to answer even if what you want to do seems okay in your eyes. You may want to start seeing results immediately but these things happen gradually. You will learn patience when you understand that you are only the vessel and the message is not your own. Don't be rash in taking key decisions, make your judgement prayerfully. Not only do you need patience in seeing your dreams and God's will fulfilled, you'll also need this in dealing with people.

If you notice that you have an impatient character, it's time to practise patience. Yes, you can practise it. Identify the things or circumstances that cause you to be impatient. You don't necessarily completely avoid them; rather you need to practise patience through them. When you're faced with them again, take a deep breath and let your mind be aligned to the workings of God's spirit. Make yourself wait. Delayed gratification is a good way for you to teach yourself patience.

15. Do not stay idle

"Idle hands are the devil's workshop; idle lips are his mouthpiece." - Proverbs 16:27, TLB

If you are going to be productive with your assignment is, you cannot afford to be idle for long. And no, you don't always have to be busy all the time – it's not healthy. Being idle is the state of lazing around or the state of just not having enough to do. Is it not funny how we complain about lack of time, yet we find time to laze around?

In overcoming idleness, the first thing to do is to plan what you want to achieve each day. If you want to relax, let it be in your plan (as long as that is what you set out to do; idleness creeps on you when you did not plan to be 'idle') and if you want to achieve tangible things, let it be in your plan for the day. With idleness, you waste your time without realizing that this is what you are doing.

The next thing to do to reduce idle time is to be sensitive about idleness throughout your day. If you are aware of something, it is easier for you to put it under check. Watch out for idle time and how it creeps on you. Let's say for example that you're trying to complete a task and then you realize that you have mentally checked out or the more common one - you have grabbed your phone to scroll through a feed. If you're conscious about your idle time, you will probably notice this within a couple of minutes but if not, you'd have spent almost an hour doing nothing. At that point, best course of action is to go back to what you were doing before you became distracted or if you truly need a break, take it.

****

If you've come to the end of this book, you are a champ! I hope that it blessed you! Ultimately, I pray that you realize what a gift you are to this world, and continually live in the fullness of the potential you carry!

*******THE END*******